THE EFFECTIVENESS OF READING RECC PHONOLOGICAL TRAINING FOR CHILDREN WITH READING PROBLEMS

FULL REPORT

THOMAS CORAM RESEARCH UNIT

PROFESSOR K. SYLVA
DR J. HURRY

with statistical consultation from

I. PLEWIS

Report prepared for
School Curriculum and Assessment Authority

1995

ACKNOWLEDGEMENTS

This study involved 120 schools and seven LEAs. In each LEA, the Reading Recovery tutor, teacher, class teacher and school administrators were asked to do a great deal above and beyond the call of duty. We are indebted to them all for their assistance, so cheerfully given. The study also required the work of five Research Officers/Tutors: Pauline Doxford, Lesley Fox-Lee, Belinda Kennedy, Helen Mirelman, and Lesley Zuke, who helped in the piloting and design of the study, completed much of the testing and trained the children on the Phonological Intervention with enthusiasm and persistence. The research owes a great deal to their intelligence and tenacity.

We are indebted to Morag McLean and Claire Kirtley for designing the training course for the Phonological Intervention and to Angela Hobsbaum for her advice and information on the Reading Recovery programme.

We also wish to thank Sheila Field who handled the administration of the project so thoroughly, and Catherine Kerrigan who so competently typed the final report. In addition, we wish to acknowledge the useful and practical guidance of the Steering Committee and especially that of the SCAA Professional Officer, Dr Sue Horner, who kept us on course with a light and humorous hand.

Professor Kathy Sylva
Dr Jane Hurry
Thomas Coram Research Unit
London, January 1995

CONTENTS

Page Number

CHAPTER 1	**RATIONALE FOR THE RESEARCH**	1
1.1	**Introduction**	1
1.2	**Background: the case for early intervention**	1
1.2.1	The traditional approach to remedial teaching	1
1.2.2	Early identification of children with reading difficulties	2
1.2.3	The consequences of reading problems for children's learning	2
1.2.4	Early intervention versus remediation at a later stage	4
1.3	**Characteristics of the interventions**	5
1.3.1	The breadth of the approach	5
1.3.2	Programmes with a phonological focus: a special case	6
1.3.3	Early interventions: they do not all work	9
1.3.4	The quality of instruction	10
1.3.5	How long do children maintain their gains?	11
1.4	**The long term effects of reading difficulties**	12
1.5	**Conclusion**	13
1.6	**Aims of the research study**	13
CHAPTER 2	**THE INTERVENTIONS**	15
2.1	**Reading Recovery**	15
2.1.1	Reading Recovery: the development	15
2.1.2	Reading Recovery: the model of reading and learning	16
2.1.3	Reading Recovery: selection, structure of the sessions, and discontinuation	17
2.1.4	Reading Recovery: teachers and tutors	19
2.2	**Phonological Intervention**	20
2.2.1	The Bryant and Bradley Intervention	20
2.2.2	Bryant and Bradley's findings	21
2.2.3	The Phonological Intervention in the present study	22
2.2.4	Training staff to administer Phonological Intervention	22
2.3	**Conclusion**	22
CHAPTER 3	**RESEARCH METHODS**	24
3.1	**Sampling**	24
3.1.1	Schools sampled	24
3.1.2	Children in the sample	25
3.2	**Research design**	26
3.3	**Measures at pre-test and follow-up**	28
3.3.1	Reading and Phonological measures	28
3.3.2	IQ measure	31

3.3.3	Measure of ability with numbers	31
3.3.4	Training staff to administer the tests	31
3.3.5	Measure of behaviour problems	31
3.3.6	Background information collected on the children	31
3.3.7	Extra help with reading: data collected	32
3.3.8	The classroom/school reading environment	32

CHAPTER 4   CHARACTERISTICS OF THE SAMPLE AND THE MEASURES OF READING AND PHONOLOGICAL AWARENESS   33

4.1	**Characteristics of the different boroughs participating in the study**	33
4.2	**Characteristics of the measures of reading and phonological awareness used**	35
4.3	**Differences between the experimental groups at the beginning of the study**	38
4.4	**Conclusion**	39

CHAPTER 5   THE EFFECTS OF READING RECOVERY AND THE PHONOLOGICAL INTERVENTION ON CHILDREN'S PROGRESS IN READING AND THEIR PHONOLOGICAL AWARENESS   40

5.1	**Reading Recovery**	40
5.1.1	How effectiveness is assessed	40
5.1.2	Progress in the first year (The Intervention Year)	41
5.1.3	Progress in the second year (when no intervention was given)	43
5.2	**Phonological Intervention**	45
5.2.1	Progress in the first year (The Intervention Year)	45
5.2.2	Progress in the second year (when no intervention was given)	48
5.3	**Differences between schools**	49
5.4	**Conclusion**	50

CHAPTER 6   THE CONTRIBUTION OF SOCIAL FACTORS, BEHAVIOURAL PROBLEMS AND INTELLIGENCE TO READING PROGRESS AND THEIR INFLUENCE ON THE EFFECTIVENESS OF THE INTERVENTIONS   51

6.1	**Factors which have a general effect on reading progress**	51
6.1.1	Poverty	53

6.1.2	English as a second language	54
6.1.3	IQ	54
6.1.4	Absence from school	55
6.1.5	Gender	55
6.1.6	Behaviour problems	55
6.2	**The characteristics of children who particularly benefit from either intervention**	56
6.2.1	The interaction between uptake of free school meals and Reading Recovery	56
6.2.2	The interaction between uptake of free school meals and the Phonological Intervention	59
6.2.3	Other interaction effects	59
6.3	**Conclusion**	59
CHAPTER 7	**CHILDREN WHO FAIL TO MAKE PROGRESS ON THE INTERVENTIONS**	60
7.1	**Reading Recovery**	60
7.2	**Children who were non-readers at the beginning of the study**	61
7.2.1	The benefits of Reading Recovery for non-readers	62
7.2.2	The benefits of the Phonological Intervention for non-readers	64
7.3	**Conclusion**	67
CHAPTER 8	**THE COST EFFECTIVENESS OF READING RECOVERY AS COMPARED WITH OTHER FORMS OF READING SUPPORT**	68
8.1	**Specialised reading help at school level**	68
8.1.1	Amount of specialised reading help given	68
8.1.2	The cost of additional reading tuition: the teacher	72
8.1.3	Effectiveness of specialised help	73
8.1.4	The length of the Reading Recovery programme	75
8.2	**Reading Recovery: discontinuation**	75
8.3	**Children with statements of special educational needs**	76
8.4	**Teacher training costs**	77
8.5	**Management at LEA level**	78
8.6	**Conclusion**	80

| CHAPTER 9 | THE SCHOOL ENVIRONMENT | 82 |

9.1	The classroom environment: information collected	82
9.2	Reading Recovery	82
9.2.1	The effect of Reading Recovery on the teaching of reading in the classroom	82
9.2.2	The effect of Reading Recovery on children's reading progress in the classroom	84
9.3	The effect of the Phonological Intervention on the teaching of reading in the classroom	86
9.4	Conclusion	86

| CHAPTER 10 | THE EFFECTS OF READING RECOVERY ON AREAS OF CHILDREN'S BEHAVIOUR OTHER THAN READING | 89 |

10.1	Behaviour problems	89
10.1.1	Measurement of children's behaviour problems	90
10.1.2	The effect of Reading Recovery on children's behaviour problems	90
10.2	School absence	91
10.3	Mathematics	91
10.4	Conclusion	92

| CHAPTER 11 | SUMMARY AND CONCLUSION | 93 |

| REFERENCES | | i |

| APPENDIX 1 | Demetre, J. D. (1993) 'A Review of Evaluation Studies of the Reading Recovery Programme', *Report for National Curriculum Council* | I |

| APPENDIX 2 | Phonological Intervention Training Manual | XVII |

| APPENDIX 3 | Tables | XXI |

| APPENDIX 4 | Multi-level modelling | XXII |

CHAPTER 1

RATIONALE FOR THE RESEARCH

1.1 Introduction

This report presents the findings of a two year longitudinal evaluation of the effectiveness of two different interventions, designed to help 6 year olds who have made a slow start in their reading. The two interventions studied, both delivered in a one-to-one setting, were Reading Recovery and a specifically phonological and less intensive programme (Phonological Training). Almost 400 children from seven local authorities participated in the evaluation: Bexley, Greenwich, Hammersmith and Fulham, Islington, Surrey, Wandsworth, and Westminster. These authorities offer a diverse sample of children in terms of socio-economic status and home circumstances, although inner-city children are over-represented in terms of the national picture.

1.2 Background: the case for early intervention

The importance of investigating ways of helping young children who are struggling with reading is to some degree self-evident. Reading problems in childhood can cause distress to children and their parents, having an impact on children's self-esteem.[1] As children progress through schooling, reading difficulties will affect their ability to participate in many classroom activities, limiting their progress not only in English but in other subject areas.

1.2.1 The traditional approach to remedial teaching

Traditionally, children have not been offered additional help with reading problems until they have been in the school system for several years. It is clear from the work of Gipps and her colleagues (1987), in their survey of 'Warnock's Eighteen Per Cent', that British children in the first half of the 1980s were normally offered remedial help only when they reached Junior school (age 7 or 8 years), two to three years after the start of formal schooling. However, there is a growing body of evidence to suggest that intervention should be offered at an earlier stage if it is to be effective.

The reluctance to intervene at an early stage stems largely from the belief that it is not possible to identify children who are going to have intractable problems with reading until they have had several years schooling. Such children are virtually non-readers in their first year or two at school, and therefore not suitable for standard reading tests, making reliable identification difficult. It has also been argued that, even if they can be identified, they might just be 'late developers' who will mature eventually.

---

[1] Johnston & Winograd, 1985, Butkowsky & Willows, 1980.

1.2.2 Early identification of children with reading difficulties

It is true that standard reading tests are not suitable for the poorer readers in their first year or two of schooling. However, assessment using pre-reading tasks involving letter recognition, an examination of children's concepts about print,[2] or phonological awareness, can discriminate well between children of 5 and 6 years and are also highly predictive of their subsequent progress with reading.[3] It is now possible to identify children with problems at an early stage, and for many of these children these problems will persist without intervention.

1.2.3 The consequences of reading problems for children's learning

The negative consequences of reading problems are likely to increase with time. Early reading problems can initiate a causal chain of effects. Very quickly, poorer readers encounter less text than their peers. Biemiller (1977)[4] has documented that these large differences in reading experience begin to emerge as early as the middle of Year 1 (mean age 6 years old). In October, the children in the three most able groups in his sample read a mean of 12.2 words per child per reading session, the children in three average ability groups read 11.9 words per child per reading session, and the children in the two least able groups were not reading. By January, the mean for the most able groups was 51.9, for the average ability groups was 25.8, and for the least able groups, 11.5. In April, the respective means were 81.4, 72.3, and 31.6. This of course says nothing about differences in home reading, which would probably be at least as large. By the time these children reach the middle primary years it has been estimated that the least motivated children might read 100,000 words a year, while the average reader might encounter 1,000,000 words of text. The more voracious readers might read as many as 10,000,000 words.[5]

The situation for poorer readers is exacerbated by the fact that they are often given books to read that are too difficult for them.[6] The problem with reading difficult texts is that children must invest too much of their mental energy on word-recognition. This leaves them few resources to allocate to understanding the sense of what they read.[7] Yet much

---

[2] Their knowledge of the most basic aspects of print, eg that print carries a message, that we read from left to right, the difference between a word and a letter, etc.

[3] Bond & Dykstra, 1967; Bryant & Bradley, 1985; Tizard et al, 1988; Lundberg et al, 1980; Calfee, 1977.

[4] See also Allington, 1980, 1983, 1984.

[5] Nagy & Anderson, 1984.

[6] Allington, 1977, 1983, 1984; Bristow, 1985; Forell, 1985; Gambrell, Wilson & Gantt, 1981; Jorgenson, 1977.

[7] LaBerge & Samuels, 1974; Perfetti, 1985; Stanovich, 1980.

of the empirical evidence indicates that children rely considerably on syntax and meaning rather than decoding skills to support their reading in the early stages of their learning. If the text is too difficult children simply cannot follow the meaning and they lack the decoding skills to read the material without understanding. The amount children understand when reading a passage is directly related to the amount of difficulty they experience in reading it. High error rates in text reading are negatively correlated with comprehension; low error rates are positively correlated with comprehension.[8] An additional problem with over-demanding books is that they create an unrewarding reading experience for children, intensifying their feelings of inadequacy and increasing their tendency to avoid such an experience in future or encouraging them to become passive learners. On the other hand books which are too easy fail to stretch children's skill.

As word reading skill develops, more general language skills become the limiting factor on reading ability.[9] But the greater reading experience of the better reader has provided an enormous advantage even here. Reading itself is an important contributor to the development of many language and cognitive skills. For example, much vocabulary growth probably takes place through the learning of word meanings from context during reading.[10] Similarly, much general information and knowledge about more complex syntactic structures probably also takes place through reading itself.[11] In short, much that facilitates further growth in reading comprehension ability – general knowledge, vocabulary, syntactic knowledge – is developed by reading. These feedback effects appear to be potent sources of individual differences in academic achievement.[12]

Children who experience repeated failure in reading also become demoralised and this influences their self-esteem and may cause them to approach future learning tasks in negative, passive and inefficient ways.[13] Poor reading may even lead to a drop in IQ. It is well established that performance on intelligence tests correlates with reading achievement. This correlation is usually in the range of 0.3 to 0.5 in the first years of schooling but rises to the range of 0.6 or 0.75 in adult samples.[14] Stanovich (1986) describes the risks to poor readers of experiencing an ever more impoverished learning environment in a thoughtful and scholarly article entitled 'Matthew effects in reading' after a quotation from the *Gospel According to Matthew*:

---

[8] Rosenshine & Stevens, 1984.

[9] Chall, 1983; Sticht, 1979.

[10] Nagy & Anderson, 1984; Nagy, Herman & Anderson, 1985; Sternberg, 1985.

[11] Donaldson & Reid, 1982; Mann, 1986; Perfetti, 1985, pp. 172-173, 195.

[12] Walberg et al, 1984.

[13] For a discussion see Johnston & Winograd, 1985.

[14] Stanovich et al, 1984.

> 'For unto everyone that hath shall be given, and he shall have abundance: but from him that hath not shall be taken away even that which he hath.' (XXV:29)

On the same theme, Chall (1983) has written:

> 'The influence of the development of reading and writing – 'literate intelligence' – on general cognitive development has unfortunately been underestimated. Indeed, when reading development is delayed by personal or environmental factors, or both, the effects on the person, unless given special help, are too often disastrous.' (pp2–3)

In a highly literate society the consequences of illiteracy can be very marked.

1.2.4 Early intervention versus remediation at a later stage

The research evidence suggests that, for reading difficulties, early intervention appears to be more effective than remediation at a later stage.

Barbara Tizard, Ian Plewis and some colleagues[15] have looked at inner-city children's progress in both reading, writing and maths during Key Stage 1. They found that the amount of progress children made depended to a significant extent on the school attended. This confirms the important contribution that schooling makes to attainment, already identified in secondary and junior schools in the UK. In fact, Tizard and her colleagues report that whereas parents *had a big influence* on the level of pre-school attainments, factors in the school were more important once the children started at infant school. Particularly relevant in the current context was their finding that the difference between schools was most marked in the reception year for reading. There are several American studies which point to the same conclusion, that the foundation of long term academic success is built in the early years when basic skills are being acquired and that it is at this time that schools may have their strongest effects.[16]

Evaluations of interventions for children with reading problems carried out in the 1970s and early 1980s are on the whole rather disappointing, rarely finding evidence of any significant lasting improvements in reading.[17] This may be due in part to the fact that during this era older children were normally targeted. Research has found that remediation of reading problems in older children is largely ineffective.[18] Another

---

[15] Tizard, Blatchford, Burke, Farquhar & Plewis, 1988.

[16] Meyer, 1984; New Study, 1983; Entwisle & Hayduk, 1982; Lazer et al, 1977.

[17] Maughan et al, 1985; Gittelman & Feingold, 1983.

[18] Carter, 1984; Juel, 1988; Kennedy, Birman & Demaline, 1986. Note, however, reports of a successful intervention by Shaver & Nuhn, 1971, and some limited success reported by Gittelman & Feingold, 1983.

reason for failure was that remedial interventions of the 1970s and early 1980s tended to be based on explanations of reading difficulties that we now know to be inaccurate, frequently placing rather too much emphasis on perceptual training (eg poor readers being given eye movement training[19]).

However, there has been greater success with younger children in their first year or two of school. It may be that it is easier to *prevent* reading problems in the first place than to attempt to remediate them further up the school. Wasik and Slavin (1993) have recently reviewed one-to-one tutoring for preventing early reading failure. They looked at 16 separate studies of five different tutoring methods, all carried out in the USA, and found children's reading to be improved in nearly every case.

1.3 Characteristics of the interventions

1.3.1 The breadth of the approach

The interventions in Wasik and Slavin's critical review were Reading Recovery, Success for All, Prevention of Learning Disabilities, Wallach Tutoring Program, and Programmed Tutorial Reading. The five tutoring programmes varied enormously in their models of reading, curriculum, tutoring methods, education and integration with regular classroom instruction. The studies were equally diverse in populations, measures, and procedures. However, the authors felt able to make some general observations:

'First, programs with the most comprehensive models of reading, and therefore the most complete instructional interventions, appear to have larger impacts than programs that address only a few components of the reading process. Reading Recovery and Success for All include in reading instruction several components of reading such as perceptual analysis, conventions of print, error correction strategies, decoding, comprehension, error detection, and reading strategies. Moreover, they have comprehensive approaches to teaching the complex process of reading. In contrast, the Prevention of Learning Disabilities program which focuses only on building specific skills related to the reading process produced less consistent comprehension outcomes.' (p196)

This observation, that broader programmes tend to produce broader effects on children's reading, fits well with information from other sources. Direct Instruction, another American intervention, was developed to help children at the beginning of their school career. The originators of this programme believed that gains made by students in Head Start could be reinforced and enhanced by a systematic three or four year programme for the first years of formal schooling.[20] The curriculum methods in the domain of reading (DISTAR) rely heavily on a word building, phonic approach and have been exported to the UK where they are used in several London secondary schools in a remedial setting. Direct Instruction is delivered to groups of children, not one-to-one, and there is some

---

[19] Allington, 1982; Arter & Jenkins, 1979; Kavale & Mattson, 1983.

[20] Becker & Gersten, 1982; Meyer, 1984.

evidence of its success both in the short and the longer term. However, the measurable effects of this programme were found in word reading and decoding skills and not in reading comprehension, similar to Wasik & Slavin's report on the Prevention of Learning Disabilities programme quoted above. In general, interventions with a narrow focus are in greater danger of missing their target, either because of the inadequacy of their model of reading (as was the case with studies involving perceptual training previously discussed) or because they are only effective for a limited range of children, or a limited range of skills.

1.3.2 Programmes with a phonological focus: a special case

On the basis of current knowledge it seems likely that if there is a specific cause of reading disability at all, it resides in the area of phonological awareness.[21] It is now fairly clear that reading progress is greater where there is explicit phonics teaching in the classroom than where there is not. Marilyn Adams (1990) undertook an extensive review of the role of phonics in early reading instruction for the US Department of Education. A fairly consistent picture emerged in her thoughtful review. It relied in particular on two major pieces of work, one by Chall (1967), who visited more than 300 infant classrooms in the USA, England and Scotland, and one by Pflaum and her colleagues (1980) who examined a selection of 655 studies cited in the *Annual Summary of Investigations Relating to Reading*. Systematic, explicit phonics instruction was associated with effective teaching methods in both these investigations. Adams concludes that the broad evidence for the importance of systematic phonics teaching in the early instruction of reading is overwhelming. However, she also remarks that virtually every reading programme teaches phonics at some level, a conclusion reached by HMI[22] in the UK as well. The distinction is generally one of emphasis and the issue translates from 'what' to 'how much' and 'in what context'.

Another aspect of successful methods of teaching reading identified by both Chall (1967) and Pflaum and her colleagues (1980) was the way in which the curriculum was taught. Both observed that a major factor in the success of any programme was the enthusiasm with which it was taught. Greater reading gains were observed when an instruction was delivered by a teacher who advocated that method and this is an important point that we will return to later on. Adams concludes 'there can be no such thing as a universal method' (p423) but that recommendations for classes of programmes emerge, namely those that embed code (phonics) instruction in a comprehensive reading programme that includes a wider range of reading activities. The importance of teaching the phonics element in the context of a good reading programme is stressed and Adams devotes considerable space in her book to making the reasons for this clear. The main points made by Adams and others in support of a wide reading programme can be summarised.

---

[21] Stanovich, 1986; Frith, 1985; Jorm et al, 1983; Goswami & Bryant, 1990.

[22] DES, 1991.

Beginning readers rely on context, amongst other things, to help them identify words. Ultimately, as mature readers, they will have memorised the vast majority of the words they read.[23] Whilst they are learning it is necessary for them to make the correct associations between the words on the page and the words in their head. Anything which allows them to do this on their own acts as a 'built-in teacher', permitting children to become independent readers. The supporting context of good reading material, well matched to children's skill, encourages such independent reading, increasing the number of positive learning trials.

Beyond this, reading books is a pleasurable activity and as such can offer children the motivation they need to attend to what they are being taught and to participate actively. Books also give a purpose to the reading, a further source of motivation and a necessary element of children taking some charge of their own reading. Motivated children will look at books and words much more frequently than the reluctant ones that only read when pressed by an alert adult. This again increases children's opportunity to make connections between the words on the page and the words in their heads.

Children's experience of reading goes far beyond the classroom. They may have come to school with a considerable knowledge of the conventions and uses of print and they will certainly go on to encounter many forms of written material, all with a purpose to convey some meaning. The richnesses of this reading environment can only help children in their journey towards literacy and it would be foolish in the extreme not to exploit it. As children's reading progresses they will certainly require a wider range of skills than those of phonics, however important. Modern psychological theory stresses the importance of embedding any learning experience of children into the wider social world that they inhabit.[24] Reading is no exception to this.

A particular example of why it is important to offer phonic instruction in a broad context is given by Tunmer[25] who discusses the pitfalls of the 'skill and drill' approach. Although our written language is in an alphabetic form it is not invariably phonetically regular. Some words, such as DOWN and BLOWN share similar spelling patterns but sound differently. Other words such as LIGHT and BITE sound the same but are spelt differently. Children need to be given enough information to make sense of this diversity. Tunmer (1994) describes this as a 'meta-cognitive' approach, Gaskins and colleagues (1988) as a 'set for diversity'.

Research carried out in the north of England illustrates the importance of placing phonic instruction in a wider reading context.[26] In this study, 7 year old children who were poor readers were divided into four matched groups and assigned to one of three experimental

---

[23] Eg Jorm et al, 1983.

[24] Eg Bruner, 1987.

[25] Tunmer, 1994.

[26] Hatcher, Hulme & Ellis, 1994.

teaching conditions: Reading with Phonology, Reading Alone, Phonology Alone, and a Control. Each programme involved the children being taught individually for 40 x 30-minute sessions spread over 20 weeks. Teachers were given a three day training in the instructional methods for each condition. The Reading package was modelled on the work of Clay (1985). The phonological training was based on contemporary understanding of children's phonological development and included work with rhyme, identification and manipulation of syllables and various other aspects of sound awareness. The Reading and Phonology training was a synthesis of the two. Although the Phonology Alone group showed most improvement on phonological tasks, the Reading with Phonology group made most progress in reading. The authors interpreted this to show that boosted phonological skills need to be integrated with the teaching of reading if they are to be maximally effective in improving literacy skills.

However, there is also evidence that early training in phonological awareness alone can have an impact on children's reading. In Denmark 235 children aged 6 years old received such a phonological training daily for nine months.[27] This did improve their phonic skills, as compared to a control group. Their spelling also benefited significantly a few months after the end of the programme, but not their reading (though there was a tendency for the experimental children to read better). However, after a further year in school the children who had received the phonological training were both spelling and reading significantly better than controls, though reading was measured with word recognition, and not text comprehension.

Another influential study of the value of phonological awareness was that of Bradley and Bryant (1985). The training for infant school pupils was based on their results with pre-schoolers. They had found that these young children had a natural facility with rhyme and that by developing this teachers could improve the children's subsequently acquired reading and spelling abilities. They were curious to see if similar techniques could help children who had very poor phonological awareness. They selected 65 six year old children who had performed very badly in pre-school tests of phonological ability. One sub-group was given individual training in various elements of sound awareness (initial sounds, rhyme, with short and long vowels, end sounds, etc) over a two year period. Another group was given a broader training that included plastic letters to help children link the sound with spelling patterns. At the end of the two year period, the children who had received the broader training were reading significantly better than the matched control group while the narrower intervention was less effective.[28]

Research results are conflicting. The success of phonological training in the Danish study and the Oxfordshire study of Bradley and Bryant is at odds with its apparent failure to improve children's reading in the Hatcher study (op. cit.). The reason for the discrepancy may be the timing of the follow-up testing. In the Danish study phonological training had an immediate effect on spelling, but only improved reading one year later.

---

[27] Lundberg, Frost & Petersen, 1988.

[28] This study, which is of great significance for the the current study, is described more fully in Chapter 2.

Uta Frith (1985) has argued that children first use phonic strategies to spell, and that their reading is initially heavily reliant on whole word recognition. She suggests that as children's understanding of the link between alphabet and the written word develops through spelling it subsequently helps them in their reading. This offers an explanation for the Danish study and is consistent with the findings of Bradley and Bryant in which children had received their intervention approximately two years before post-test. If the influence of phonological intervention on reading works largely through its effects on spelling, gains in reading may take longer to show. The effect of the Bradley and Bryant intervention was more obvious in the children's spelling than in their reading.

1.3.3 Early interventions: they do not all work

Wasik and Slavin (1993) observed in their review of one-to-one tutoring programmes that not all of these interventions were successful.

> 'It is not enough that programs simply use more tutors. The content of the reading program, in addition to the form of instructional delivery may be important variables. Ellison et al (1968), for example, found the Programmed Tutorial Reading model to be significantly more effective than a standard "direct tutoring" intervention, and Arnold et al (1977) found the Prevention of Learning Disabilities (TEACH) program to be considerably more effective than "regular tutoring". Mantzicopoulos et al (1990) failed to replicate the findings of earlier studies of Prevention of Learning Disabilities, but similarly found few effects of a "standard" phonics-based tutoring approach. An Ohio statewide study of Reading Recovery failed to find any positive effects of two alternative models of one-to-one tutoring (Pinnell et al, 1991).'[29]

In the Hatcher study described earlier,[30] only children taught the Reading and Phonology programme benefited significantly from individual tuition. Those who received 40 half hour sessions on either a Reading alone programme or a Phonology alone programme were not substantially better off than children who had received nothing but classroom instruction.

Early interventions offered in a group setting have also been found to be of questionable effectiveness. In a very influential British study Tizard et al (1981) measured the effect on the reading of 6 to 8 year olds of having their parents listen to them read regularly at home. This was found to improve their reading, compared with a control group. In the same study, as a comparison, extra reading tuition at school was provided by a specialist teacher who worked with the children on a small group basis, seeing each child several times a week for a two year period. The children given extra reading tuition at school did not make significantly greater progress than the control children. In a very wide-ranging

---

[29] Wasik & Slavin, 1993, p. 196.

[30] Hatcher et al, 1994.

American study of compensatory education in primary school[31] Carter reported that such interventions were most effective at improving the reading of children in the first grade (our Year 1), but that they were, by no means, invariably successful. Compensatory education was more effective for moderately disadvantaged children than for the most disadvantaged. In another American review of Chapter 1 services Kennedy and her colleagues (1986) report similar findings. In the Pinnell evaluation of Reading Recovery one group of poor readers were given group instruction by fully trained Reading Recovery teachers. They failed to make significantly more progress than the control group.

1.3.4 The quality of instruction

Beyond content, the effectiveness of any intervention depends on the quality of implementation, an obvious fact which is nonetheless overlooked. We mentioned earlier that it has been a consistent finding that children learn more when they are taught by an enthusiastic and motivated teacher.[32] It is correct to refer to the 'art of teaching', since what is learnt goes beyond the bare bones of what is taught, important though this is. It is also dependent on how captivated is the pupil by the art of the teacher.

Some aspects of programme delivery are open to influence. Teaching experience, training and a belief in the advocated method of teaching can all improve implementation. In their large review of reading method studies, Pflaum and colleagues (1980) found that in three-quarters of those studies the experimental group was superior to its control. One of the reasons for the effectiveness of anything new is that it tends to be taught with optimism and enthusiasm. In a well designed evaluation of a successful phonically oriented intervention the authors specifically comment:

> 'The fact that we excluded children with clear behavioural problems may lead to the erroneous impression that the youngsters were eager to co-operate. Quite to the contrary, most were willing victims at best, and obtaining their active involvement was of concern in many cases. The reinforcement made a tremendous difference in obtaining the children's co-operation. This difference does much, in turn, for the morale of the teachers and it cannot be assumed that progress such as that obtained in this study can be accomplished with a less vigorous teaching programme or with less enthusiastic staff'. (Gittelman and Feingold, 1983, p188)

Breadth of training does seem to be important. Wasik and Slavin (1993) found that programmes using qualified teachers as tutors appeared to obtain substantially larger impacts than those using paraprofessionals. Effect sizes for the programmes they reviewed which were delivered by paraprofessionals generally fell in the range of +0.2 to

---

[31] Carter, 1984. Data was collected on 120,000 students.

[32] Chall, 1967, and Pflaum et al, 1980.

+0.75 while those for the programmes using certified teachers produced average effects from +0.55 to +2.37.

This leads us to the second concern regarding the implementation of programmes: the degree to which they are taught as designed. It is rare for research studies to address this issue. It is a *sine qua non* in most evaluations that the programme being studied is taught with precision and, this is as it should be, for it would be foolish to evaluate an intervention that only poorly reflected the initial design. However, little thought is usually given to the maintenance of authenticity. As a result there is very little evidence concerning the effect of programme drift. Gittelman & Feingold (op. cit.) remarked that classroom teachers were resentful of their intervention, implemented by researchers hired specifically for the purpose. Where this is perfectly acceptable for a piece of empirical research it does raise the question of how such an intervention could be successfully implemented in the real world. The failure of Mantzicopoulos and colleagues (1990) to replicate the findings of the earlier studies of Prevention of Learning Disabilities may have been due to the fact that the programme was delivered in a different way.[33] No information on implementation was collected. In contrast, Reading Recovery addresses both the issue of the quality of teacher instruction and the maintenance of the programme integrity. This is described more fully in Chapter 2, in the section dealing with Reading Recovery.

1.3.5 How long do children maintain their gains?

Because tutoring children is expensive (especially on a one-to-one basis), its lasting effects are of great importance, but despite this, few follow-up studies have been carried out. There is a tendency for remedial programmes to lead to short term gains only.[34] Follow-up studies of Direct Instruction, a widely implemented intervention in the USA, have found that the children lost ground after the programme ended, failing, for example, to develop their vocabularies and reading comprehension.[35] A one year follow-up of Prevention of Learning Disabilities showed improved scores for word identification and word attack skills, but the effects for reading comprehension decreased one year after the intervention.[36]

Some evaluations do not test children's reading attainment but report long term referral rates to specialist services. Two of the studies reviewed by Wasik & Slavin (1993): Success for All and Programmed Tutorial Reading, document substantial reductions in the numbers of children being kept back for a year as a result of early one-to-one intervention, and Success for All also showed reductions in special educational referrals,

---

[33] See Wasik & Slavin, 1993, p.193.

[34] Carroll, 1972; Kennedy et al, 1986.

[35] Becker & Gersten, 1982; Meyer, 1984. The same was found to be true for maths: Gersten & Carnine, 1984.

[36] Silver, Hagin & Beecher, 1981.

but, the use of subsequent uptake of remedial services as a measure of programme effectiveness is problematic. If an intervention is embedded in the education system it may have implications for the funding of different arms of the same service and so money made available for one intervention may reduce the amount available for other specialist services. It is also possible that early identification of reading problems may increase early referrals to specialist services for children who would otherwise only have appeared much later in the system. Service provision is not a reliable measure of the amount or severity of reading problems.

Reading Recovery has been evaluated for lasting effects in two main ways. Several studies have looked at whether or not children who have been through Reading Recovery fall within the average band of readers in subsequent years.[37] In general, they have reported that such children do fall comfortably within the normal range. However, some of these studies only consider children who have *successfully* completed Reading Recovery, which limits their power. If the children with extreme reading difficulties who do not successfully complete the programme are excluded from the experimental group, a fair test of the intervention has not been carried out.

A large scale American study compared Reading Recovery children with controls in a long term follow-up.[38] Reading Recovery children maintained their text reading-level advantage over the comparison children for three years after completing the intervention.

From the earlier discussion of the ever widening effects of reading problems it might be expected that successful early interventions should have long lasting effects. The evidence is limited because of the paucity of studies but there seems to be reason for cautious optimism, with the proviso that children may fail to make progress in areas that were not originally addressed in the intervention (for example, reading comprehension under Direct Instruction).

1.4 The long term effects of reading difficulties

The Adult Literacy and Basic Skills Unit has published material put together from various sources[39] which suggests that adults who have problems with reading and writing:

> 'are more likely to be poorer than average; are more likely to be dependent on benefits; are less likely to own their own home; have fewer jobs to choose from; face longer and more frequent periods of unemployment'.

---

[37] See the appended report by Demetre, 1993, for further details.

[38] The Columbus Longitudinal Study, Pinnell et al, 1988. Data from a further year's progress is reported in Reading Recovery Program, 1991.

[39] The information reported here appears in an ALBSU, 1994, booklet entitled Basic Skills. This drew on information obtained from the Gallup Household Survey, June 1993 and from the National Childhood Development Study, ALBSU, 1987.

'There is also a clear link between basic skills and crime. Although up-to-date information is not available, in 1985/86 a report found that about 6 per cent of inmates in prison could only read as well as the average 8 year old. A further 9 per cent only had the reading ability of an average 10 year old. Among younger offenders the problems with basic skills were even worse. There is little reason to think that the position is different now.' (ALBSU, 1994, p7)

In fact interpreting the meaning of such associations is not straightforward. In particular the relationship that is known to exist between reading difficulties and lower socio-economic status and in turn between SES and adult outcome examined by ALBSU make clear conclusions difficult. However, there is strong evidence of a link between reading difficulties in primary school and subsequently poor employment history in early adult life, even after account has been taken of SES.[40]

1.5 Conclusion

We therefore conclude that preventing reading difficulties could greatly improve children's school experience and add to their success in later life. We know from cost-benefit analyses carried out by the developers of High/Scope[41] that this success can be translated into considerable financial benefits for society as a whole, for example, by reducing the numbers of those who break the law or those on social benefits and by increasing tax revenue on income. There is strong evidence to suggest that early intervention as opposed to later remedial treatment stands the highest chance of success; but to be effective, it will require high standards of training and a reasonably extended period of intervention.[42] Programmes with a broad model of reading seem likely to produce a wider range of improvements in reading but some element of explicit phonic instruction seems advisable as well.

1.6 Aims of the research study

The main aim of the present study was to investigate practical ways of helping children in the early years of formal schooling who had made a slow start in their reading. It was decided to evaluate two programmes, both with a proven track record, but with very different approaches. The first, Reading Recovery, is one of the most successful early interventions with a broad model of reading. The second, a phonological intervention closely based on that of Bradley and Bryant,[43] is one of the most successful interventions (albeit in a research setting) with a narrower focus.

---

[40] Maughan et al, 1985; Spreen, 1978.

[41] Schweinhart & Weikart, 1993.

[42] Wasik & Slavin, 1993, discuss the evidence that the programmes they evaluated showed evidence of cumulative effects associated with programme length.

[43] Bradley & Bryant, 1985.

Bearing in mind the expensive nature of individual tuition it was decided to monitor costs as well as effectiveness. It was also deemed important to investigate whether either one of these programmes was particularly suited to certain groups of children.

CHAPTER 2

THE INTERVENTIONS

2.1 Reading Recovery

Reading Recovery is a sophisticated intervention designed to help children who are in the bottom 20 per cent of their class after one year of schooling. It is best characterised as a preventative intervention, rather than a remedial programme, as many of the children who are offered Reading Recovery are barely reading at all. The intention is to correct the inadequate strategies used by these children so that they will go on to be independent readers.

The features of Reading Recovery which mark it out as sophisticated reside not only in the programme curriculum but also in its attention to implementation issues. Clay argues[1] that to work effectively, Reading Recovery must achieve change along four dimensions:

- behavioural change on the part of teachers;
- child behaviour change achieved by teaching;
- organisational changes in schools achieved by teachers and administrators; and
- social/political changes in financing by controlling authorities.

The unusual attention to the educational system into which the programme must fit makes Reading Recovery unique, especially its in-service training and support of teachers.

2.1.1 Reading Recovery: the development

In the course of her detailed studies of how children learn to read and write, Clay designed a one-to-one tutorial intervention that was subsequently named 'Reading Recovery'. The precise nature of the programme evolved over some time as Clay worked with a team of practising teachers to develop both theory and practice.[2] For example, when the initial evaluation of the programme was carried out children only received an average of around two lessons per week.[3] This was subsequently changed to a daily programme as it was found that the children at whom the programme was aimed found it difficult to retain the lessons learnt during a session unless these were rapidly reinforced. The fact that Reading Recovery was developed in a practical school setting is important as it should make implementation easier.

---

[1] Clay, 1987.

[2] Clay, 1979, 1985, 1987.

[3] Clay, 1985.

Reading Recovery is a school-based strategy, designed and developed for implementation within the New Zealand education system, where instructional reading programmes are based on the use of graded natural language tests. It has, however, also been implemented in education systems which employ other approaches to reading instruction such as those based on a series of basal texts, as in Columbus, Ohio.

2.1.2 Reading Recovery: the model of reading and learning

According to Clay, reading is defined as a 'message-gaining, problem-solving activity which increases power and flexibility the more it is practised'.[4] She suggests that children make use of a variety of strategies to help them in this problem-solving activity, the most central of which are: their understanding of the concepts of print, their phonological awareness (both of the sounds in words and of the letters and letter strings on the page), their understanding of the meaning of the text and finally, their knowledge of syntax. Meaning is not derived from the print alone but also from the knowledge of the world that readers bring to the task, for example, their knowledge of the language of books and language in general, their prior knowledge of the subject matter of the text, their ability to make inferences. The goal of Reading Recovery is to help children to use all the skills or strategies that they have at their disposal. An important aspect of this is to encourage children to monitor their own reading, detecting and correcting errors by checking responses against all the possible strategies.

Children must be fully aware of the purpose of reading in order to develop an independent self-extending system. Thus they must frequently engage in reading connected text and should avoid working too much on isolated skills in order to become proficient in reading. This will also help readers to make use of a wider range of strategies. The larger the chunk of printed language used, the richer the network of information available to children to make sense of the text.

Reading and writing are seen as closely interconnected, writing being a particularly appropriate vehicle for developing phonic awareness in a purposeful setting, and phonic awareness then improving reading.

The teacher's role is to control carefully the texts that pupils read, ensuring that books are neither too easy nor too difficult, that the content is matched to children's interests and experience and to introduce books to children in such a way as to support the reading process. The teacher should aim to instruct children, working just beyond what children can currently do. Vygotsky[5] calls this the 'zone of proximal development', and within this zone of operations teachers can have the most impact on their pupils.

---

[4] Clay, 1979.

[5] Vygotsky, 1978, 1986.

2.1.3 Reading Recovery: selection, structure of the sessions, and discontinuation

The children who have been in school for one year (aged around 6 years old in New Zealand and the UK) and who are the poorest readers in their class are eligible for Reading Recovery. Selection is made on the basis of a battery of tests which cover concepts about print, letter identification, word reading, word writing and dictation, and text reading level.[6] The precise selection is a professional judgement, made on the basis of the child's profile of scores. It is recommended that the bottom 20 per cent of readers in the age band be offered the programme.

Once selected, children are withdrawn from their class for individual tuition daily for half an hour, until they have reached the average reading level of their classmates.

For the first two weeks the teacher and pupil 'roam around the known', reading and writing together in a supportive fashion, to build a positive relationship and to give the teacher information on which to build a structured sequence of activities.

'In Reading Recovery a typical tutoring session would include each of these activities, usually in the following order, as the format of the daily lesson:

LESSON COMPONENT	FOCUS
■ rereading two or more familiar books	text
■ rereading yesterday's new book and taking a running record	text
■ letter identification (plastic letters on a magnetic board) *and/or* word-making and breaking	words and letters
■ writing a story (including hearing and recording sounds in words)	text and sounds
■ cut-up story to be rearranged	text
■ new book introduced	text
■ new book attempted	text'[7]

The child reads familiar books. The child reads again several favourite books that s/he has previously read. The materials are storybooks with natural language rather than controlled vocabulary. Books within a lesson may range from quite easy to more challenging, but the child is generally reading above 90 per cent accuracy. During this time, the child has a chance to gain experience in fluent reading and in using strategies 'on the run' while focusing on the meaning of the text. The teacher interacts with the child during and after the reading, not 'correcting',

---

[6] Clay, 1985.

[7] Clay, 1993.

but talking with the child about the story and supporting the effective actions the child has taken.

'The teacher analyses reading by taking the running record. Each day the teacher takes a running record of a book that was new for the child the previous day. The running record is a procedure similar to miscue analysis (Goodman, Watson, & Burke, 1987). Using a kind of shorthand of checks and other symbols, the teacher records the child's reading behaviour during oral reading of the day's selected book. The teacher examines running records closely, analysing errors and paying particular attention to behaviour such as self-correction. In this way, s/he determines the strategies the child makes. While the child is reading, the teacher acts as a neutral observer; the child works independently. The accuracy check tells the teacher whether the text was well selected and introduced the day before.

'Letter identification and/or making and breaking words. Using plastic letters on a magnetic board, the teacher may take the opportunity to work briefly with the letters to increase the child's familiarity with the names of letters and their use in known words such as the child's name. This work will vary according to the knowledge the child already has.

'The child writes a story including hearing the sounds in words. Every day the child is invited to compose a message and to write it with the help of the teacher. Writing is considered an integral part of gaining control over messages in print. The process gives the child a chance to closely examine the details of written language in a message that s/he has composed, supported by her/his own language and sense of meaning. Through writing, the child also develops strategies for hearing sound in words and using visual information to monitor and check her/his reading.

'Cut-up story. After the construction of the message, the teacher writes it on a sentence strip and cuts it up for the reassemble and read. This activity provides a chance to search, check, and notice visual information.

'The child reads new books. Every day the child is introduced to a new book that s/he will be expected to read without help the next day. Before reading, the teacher talks with the child about the book as they look at the pictures. The teacher helps the child build a frame of meaning prior to reading the text. The purpose of the introduction is not necessarily to introduce new words, but to create understanding in advance of reading so that it will be easier to focus on meaning.'[8]

---

[8] Wasik & Slavin, 1993, pp.183-184.

Children graduate or are 'discontinued' from the programme when they have reached the about 'average' reading level for their class. However, it is also considered important that they should be independent readers to some extent.[9] In his report on Reading Recovery in New Zealand for OFSTED Frater remarks:

> 'Indeed, because a measure of regression must be expected on discontinuation from the scheme, it is customary to ensure that the child can work at one or two levels above that of the class group average before discontinuation occurs.'[10]

Some children fail to reach a satisfactory reading level and it is recommended that they be referred to a remedial service. In any case the maximum number of weeks recommended in the programme is between 20 and 26 weeks. The average number of weeks varies but would appear to be around 16 weeks in mature programmes.

2.1.4 Reading Recovery: teachers and tutors

Experienced teachers are selected for training as teachers or tutors. Teachers' training takes one year during which the trainees teach four pupils each, while attending weekly seminars where they acquire skill in observational, diagnostic, and assessment techniques and are taught about the mode of reading underpinning Reading Recovery. Teachers also participate in weekly 'behind the glass' demonstration lessons where they observe each other teaching behind a one-way mirror and have the opportunity to critique and discuss the lesson. Considerable time is spent learning about the reading process and learning how to implement appropriate strategies to meet the needs of individual children. Additional training is required of tutors who are certified to train and support Reading Recovery teachers in their Education Authority. The continuing support and monitoring role of the tutor is seen as crucial to maintain the quality of implementation in the post-training years.

The theory behind this extensive and powerful method of training is an extension of the learning theory applied to the child in Reading Recovery.[11] Adults also learn by integrating new knowledge into their existing view of the world, through conversation with their colleagues and more experienced mentors. Some of the theories that teachers bring to Reading Recovery are considered to be inappropriate and an important aspect of the training is to recognise this and to encourage teachers to alter their theory and practice where necessary. Beyond ensuring that Reading Recovery is taught in a precise way, considerable efforts are also made to gain teachers' enthusiastic commitment to the programme.

---

[9] This translates into reading at approximately book level 16 on Reading Recovery graded texts, Glynn et al, 1989.

[10] OFSTED, 1993, p.7.

[11] See Pinnell et al, 1994, for a discussion.

The Reading Recovery teacher training is expensive. Some argue that such extensive training is unnecessary. However, Pinnell and her colleagues (1994) found that the programme ceased to be effective when implemented by teachers who had been trained in a much shorter course. The longer course is likely to ensure a more accurate delivery of the programme and to gain the commitment of the teachers, an element which has been identified as one of the hallmarks of a successful intervention.

A full review of all the research studies which have evaluated Reading Recovery was prepared by Jim Demetre in 1993 and can be seen in Appendix 1.

2.2 Phonological Intervention

The Phonological Intervention grew out of the work of Peter Bryant and Lynette Bradley, who were interested in the observed relationship between poor phonic awareness and subsequently delayed reading.[12] In order to test the hypothesis that poor phonological awareness was one of the causal factors in children's difficulties they devised an experimental intervention consisting of a phonological training programme. It was designed for 6 year olds with poor phonic awareness, and was closely based on Lynette Bradley's experience as a teacher.[13] The circumstances surrounding the development of the Phonological Intervention differ sharply from those of Reading Recovery, hence implementation issues were not considered, beyond ensuring that the researchers delivered the intervention adequately.

2.2.1 The Bryant and Bradley Intervention

The intervention designed by Bryant and Bradley was based on their research into the normal developmental stages of phonological awareness. They had already found that pre-school children who could not read were nonetheless able both to hear and produce rhymes with evident relish. Bradley and Bryant argued that the most natural division of words into smaller sound units was that of onset and rime, i.e. 'b' + 'at'; 'r' + 'ing'. Thus their training placed emphasis on an awareness of various methods of sound categorisation, starting with rhyme and initial sounds. Its aim was to develop the awareness of sound, concentrating at the outset on alliteration and rhyme but moving towards more sophisticated phonic distinctions in response to the child's progress. Each child was given 40 10-minute, individual sessions, spread over two years. During these sessions the children were introduced to a series of pictures of familiar objects and encouraged to consider the sounds their names contained in various combinations. They were asked to say the names of the objects in a group of four or five pictures. Next they were asked to say the words again, and to listen to them. Then they were asked to say them yet again, listening to see if they could hear anything 'the same' about them.

---

[12] E.g. Bryant & Bradley, 1985; Lundberg et al, 1980.

[13] Bradley, 1984, 1981.

Typically they would be asked to identify the 'odd one out', in terms of rhyme, alliteration, etc. For example, the odd one out for the words CAT, MAT, PEN and BAT would be PEN. Children were also asked to think of examples in their heads, especially as their training progressed.

This was the pure sound awareness training. However, Bradley and Bryant felt that in order to help the children to read and write they should link the sound training to a more tangible experience of letters and spellings. Bradley had found that an effective way of showing a child how to translate sound categories into reading and spelling is to use sets of plastic letters (as are used in Reading Recovery). Bradley and Bryant write:

> 'Backward readers are often not at all successful in the aural medium, which to them seems particularly abstract and transitory. It is Bradley's experience that they are helped if, as they are being taught about sound categories, they are given something concrete and tangible to work with. The teacher uses the plastic letters to form one word, then another, and so on. All the words in the series have a sound, or more than one sound, in common, and the common sound or sounds are represented by a particular letter or letters. As the teacher finishes with one word either she or the child breaks it up, but always leaves the letter representing the sound it has in common with the next word untouched: new letters are added to it to form the next word, and then the whole process is repeated again several times. The effect is to make the relationship between the sounds that the words have in common and the letters that represent them very obvious. Alliteration and rhyme become literally tangible.'[14]

2.2.2 Bryant and Bradley's findings

In the resulting study, 65 children aged 6 years old and with poor phonological awareness were selected: 13 children were given sound awareness training, 13 children were given the same training but with plastic letters, and 26 children were trained on a control condition (conceptual categorisation), and 13 children received no training. The children who were trained in sound awareness alone did better than the control children in both reading and spelling, but this only reached statistical significance ($p < 0.05$) for the comparison with the untrained controls. The children who received the sound training with plastic letters made significantly more progress than all the control children, with reading and spelling ages at least 10 months in excess of the control groups. They did particularly well in spelling.

In a second study, Bradley[15] condensed the sound plus plastic letters intervention to 28 x 10-minute sessions, taught over 14 weeks. However, this form, although successful in

---

[14] Bradley & Bryant, 1985, p. 76.

[15] Bradley, 1988.

raising children's reading ability, failed to show lasting effects and Bradley concluded that the intervention was perhaps too condensed.

2.2.3 The Phonological Intervention in the present study

In the present study the content of the intervention was very similar to the sound and plastic letters intervention of Bradley and Bryant. However, it was not suitable to give the intervention over two years, as in the case of the original successful experiment. In the light of Bradley's experience with a condensed programme, the 40 x 10-minute sessions were retained but spread over seven months instead of two years.

2.2.4 Training staff to administer Phonological Intervention

The phonological tutors, all of whom were experienced primary teachers, were given a training package which began with a one-day training session in the techniques required to teach the Phonological Intervention, together with a training manual (Appendix 2). The tuition was given by Clare Kirtley and Morag Maclean, researchers involved in the original Bradley and Bryant studies (Bryant and Bradley, 1985; Bradley and Bryant, 1985; Kirtley et al, 1989) who administered the phonological programme in those projects. After their initial training, the research team practised teaching the Phonological Intervention to children who were not involved in the research, for one week. They then reassembled to discuss problems they had encountered and received feedback from Kirtley and Maclean. Further training sessions were held every month at the Thomas Coram Research Unit to discuss any problems concerning the intervention and queries were answered by Kirtley or Maclean by telephone contact.

Further training was given three months after the initial training session by Morag Maclean and some additions made to the training manual to take account of the more advanced activities which were required by some of the pupils making good progress. The Senior Research Officer on the project observed each member of the team teaching the Phonological Intervention to some of their children to check on the integrity of the delivery and on the standardisation. The researchers recorded the content of every lesson, for every child, to facilitate monitoring. Beyond ensuring that the phonological tutors taught the programme well the importance of gaining their commitment was also understood and every effort was made to capture their hearts as well as their minds.

2.3 Conclusion

Both the interventions being evaluated have been found to be effective in the past, though the research on Reading Recovery has been more extensive. They both have in common their target population: 6 year olds with reading problems, and the fact that they are designed for individual tuition. However, each intervention is based on a different model of reading. Reading Recovery has been developed to offer children a complete teaching programme for the initial stages of reading, whereas the Phonological Intervention offers additional tuition in a specific area, that of phonological awareness. There is no intention that the Phonological Intervention should be a self-sufficient method of teaching reading. Thus the focus of Reading Recovery is wider, and the amount of time given to each individual child greater.

The interventions also differ in the history of their development. Reading Recovery was designed for use in primary schools on a national scale, whereas the Phonological Intervention was originally designed as a part of research on the process of reading development. As a result Reading Recovery deals much more thoroughly with implementation issues and a sophisticated system has been designed to cope with training and the ongoing aspects of programme maintenance. Issues surrounding both the accuracy with which a particular programme is taught over a period of years and the commitment of the teachers involved are absolutely crucial to the practical value of that programme. However, they are frequently ignored and the attention to this aspect of intervention is a hallmark of Reading Recovery.

CHAPTER 3

RESEARCH METHODS

3.1 Sampling

3.1.1 Schools sampled

Reading Recovery programmes were evaluated in seven Local Education Authorities: Bexley, Greenwich, Hammersmith and Fulham, Islington, Surrey, Wandsworth and Westminster.[1]

In order that the Reading Recovery programme should be evaluated on the performance of established rather than trainee teachers, only schools where the Reading Recovery teachers had completed their training were included. Also, every effort was made to ensure that sampled schools were delivering Reading Recovery in the standard way. The final number of Reading Recovery schools sampled was 22.[2]

For each **Reading Recovery** school, the LEA was asked to identify two other similar schools, which were then randomly assigned to the **Control** or **Phonological Intervention** condition. Thus 23 schools were randomly assigned to the Phonological Intervention condition[3] and 18 schools were randomly assigned to the Control condition. Fewer schools in the Control category were selected as Control children were also sampled in the Reading Recovery and Phonological school.[4]

---

[1] All these authorities, with the exception of Surrey, had participated in a training course mounted by the INSET Department of the London Institute of Education, where Marie Clay was Visiting Professor. A teacher from Surrey had gone to New Zealand to train as a Reading Recovery tutor and returned to establish the programme in 1990/91.

[2] 24 such schools were identified by the LEAs and all were included in the evaluation. However, during the course of the evaluation year, two schools had to abandon Reading Recovery and were therefore dropped from the research. A further school failed to deliver the programme in the standard way, only offering twice-weekly instead of daily sessions. As all the children in this school were discontinued (deemed to have successfully completed the programme) within the year, the school is included in the results shown below, with the exception of the number of weeks children stayed in the programme. Analyses were performed with these children omitted, as a precaution, but this was found to make no difference to the results.

[3] Three further schools originally assigned to Phonological Intervention condition were dropped from the study: two from Surrey which, for geographical reasons, were impossible for a teacher of the phonological training to visit on a sufficiently frequent basis; and one from Bexley where the matched Reading Recovery school left the programme.

[4] One further school was approached for the Control condition but declined to participate.

3.1.2 Children in the sample

Initially, six children were included in the study from each selected school. The selection criteria followed those prescribed for the Reading Recovery programme. Children between the ages of 6 years and 6 years 6 months were considered. The six poorest readers in each school in this age range were identified by the class teacher and tested on the Diagnostic Survey developed for Reading Recovery. Those children in the bottom six joined the study.[5]

In the Reading Recovery schools, three or four of these bottom six readers entered the intervention programme in September and October 1992. The research team had no control over which children were selected. This decision was made by the Reading Recovery schools, ostensibly on the basis of the children's performance on the Diagnostic tests, the poorest readers being selected. Those children not selected for Reading Recovery formed the 'within school' Control group.[6]

In the Phonological schools, four of the six poorest readers in each school were randomly assigned by a member of the research team to the Phonological Intervention condition. The remaining two children formed the 'within school' Control group for the Phonological schools.[7]

Table 3.1 illustrates the number of children in each condition at pre-test, at first post-test in June/July 1993[8] and at second post-test in May/July 1994.[9]

---

[5] In two of the Surrey Reading Recovery schools it was not possible to follow these selection procedures precisely. However, the children selected were still the poorest readers in the age range.

[6] Later in the academic year a small number of those 'within school' control children were offered places on the Reading Recovery programme. If they completed the programme before or not long after the end of the Summer term 1993, they were included in the Reading Recovery group. A small group of Reading Recovery children were not considered by their teacher to have finished the programme before they were tested. These children had had a minimum of 20 weeks in the programme. They have been included in the Reading Recovery group but the analyses reported below have been performed excluding these children and have yielded very similar results.

[7] For both Reading Recovery and Phonological schools attempts were made to replace children before the end of January 1993, by testing another child, either as a control or to receive one of the interventions.

[8] Of the 17 children lost at first follow-up, 10 had to be excluded as they had been in one of the intervention conditions and had failed to receive a sufficient amount of the intervention, usually as a result of moving school. The remaining seven children, a tiny proportion of the total (2 per cent), could not be tested because they had moved too far or were impossible to trace.

[9] A further 11 children were impossible to test in May/July 1994. It was impossible to trace five children, parents refused us permission to test one child and five children had moved abroad. However, four children who could not be seen in June/July 1993 were re-contacted. Thus there was an overall loss of seven children in the year 1993/94 (2 per cent attrition.)

Table 3.1

Sample

School/Experimental condition	Number of children tested		
	Sept/Oct 1992	June/July 1993	May/July 1994
Reading Recovery Schools (22)			
Children who received RR	95	89	91[10]
Within school Control children	41	40	36
Phonological Schools (23)			
Children who received Phonological Intervention	97	91	87
Within school Control children	46	44	44
Control Schools (18)	111	109	107
Total	390	373	366

3.2 Research design

To assess the effects of any intervention, one must compare the intervention children with a similar group of Control children. One good way to select the groups is to assign children attending the same school randomly to one or other condition. Random assignment ensures that no selection bias creates systematic differences between comparison groups. Comparing children within one school ensures that their schooling, with the exception of the intervention, is similar. It has been well established that the particular school a child attends influences his/her academic performance, even when the schools being compared have a similar intake (Mortimore et al, 1988, Tizard et al, 1988).

However, there is a problem in comparing experimental and Control children attending the same school, which is frequently encountered in educational research. Where the intervention is likely to have an effect on the school's general approach to some curriculum area, which is not uncommonly the case, not only the experimental group will be affected but the Control children also. Although neither of the interventions being evaluated here are classroom based, it is part of the agenda in the UK setting to disseminate aspects of good practice encapsulated in Reading Recovery to the general teaching of reading and writing at Key Stage 1. Accordingly, quite a complex research design was necessary to make a fair test of the two interventions, using both Control children attending the same schools as Reading Recovery and Phonological children (the

---

[10] Four children changed condition in the Reading Recovery schools, from Control to Reading Recovery. These children all received Reading Recovery late in the school year 1992/93 and for a small part of the Autumn term 1993/94. For first follow-up they were tested pre-Reading Recovery.

'within school' group) and Control children attending different schools (the 'between schools' group).

It was possible to randomly assign children in the Phonological schools to the Phonological Intervention or the Control group for two reasons: 1) practically, the research team was offering this intervention as something extra and free of charge to the schools involved; and 2) ethically, it was not possible to predict which of the bottom six readers would benefit particularly from this intervention.

However, it was not possible to assign children randomly in the Reading Recovery schools to the Intervention or Control condition. As mentioned above, the Reading Recovery schools themselves wished to select which children received this intervention on the basis of their scores on the Diagnostic Survey. It is part of the Reading Recovery procedure that the children with the poorest scores should be offered the programme. Any child in the bottom six readers in the Reading Recovery schools not taken into Reading Recovery in the course of the year became part of the 'within school' Control group. They were, on average, better readers than those offered the programme, which was to be expected from the selection criteria. It should also be noted that in three of the Reading Recovery schools all of the children initially identified as Controls were ultimately offered Reading Recovery.

For both Interventions the children receiving the Intervention were also compared with control children (also poor readers) who were attending different schools. In the case of the Reading Recovery children this meant comparing them with control children in the control schools and control children in the Phonological schools. Phonological children were compared only with children in Control schools. The possibility that even control children in Reading Recovery schools might receive some benefit from the programme (sometimes called 'programme leakage') meant that they were not an ideal control group. However, for these between schools comparisons it would be necessary to take account of any systematic differences between schools, which had nothing to do with the interventions, at the point of analysis. For this reason it was necessary to have a sample size of approaching 20 schools in each condition to ensure sufficient power in statistical tests.

All the children in the study were assessed on a battery of measures (described below) in September and October 1992, before the start of tuition under one of the two interventions. The children were then retested in June and July 1993 after the interventions were completed. There was a further follow-up in May, June and July 1994. **Figure 3.1** presents the timetable of these events. Testing at both follow-up points was carried out entirely by the research team, who were unaware of ('blind') to whether or not any child had received either of the interventions.

Figure 3.1

Timetable of the research

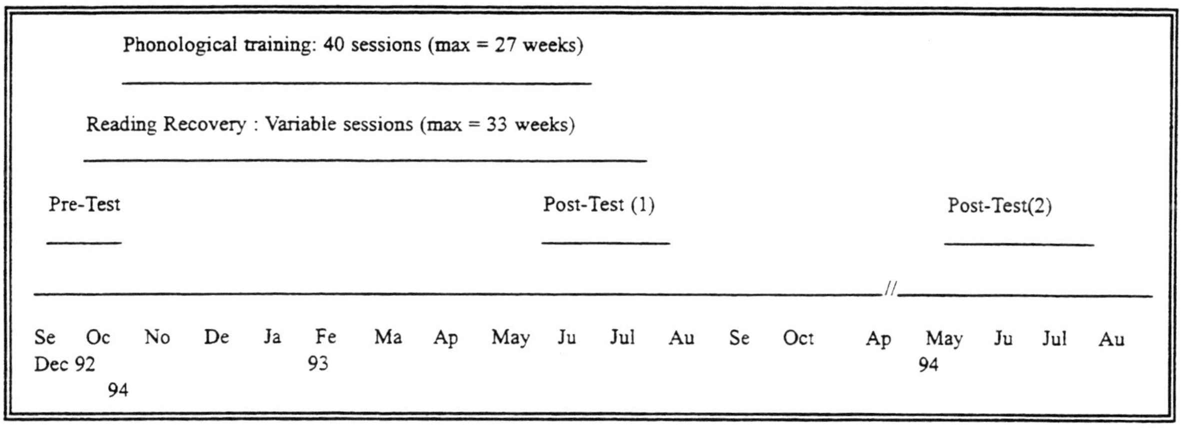

```
Phonological training: 40 sessions (max = 27 weeks)
─────────────────────────────────────────────

Reading Recovery : Variable sessions (max = 33 weeks)
─────────────────────────────────

Pre-Test                    Post-Test (1)              Post-Test(2)
────                         ────                        ────

                                                      //
─────────────────────────────────────────────────────   ──────────

Se  Oc  No  De  Ja  Fe  Ma  Ap  May  Ju  Jul  Au  Se  Oct   Ap  May  Ju  Jul  Au
Dec 92          93                                                94
    94
```

On the basis of the research design four comparisons are made in the current report as follows:

1. Phonological children with Control children in the same school ('within school' Controls)
2. Phonological children with Control children in other schools ('between school' Controls)
3. Reading Recovery children with Control children in the same school ('within school' Controls)
4. Reading Recovery children with Control children in other schools ('between school' Controls)

Analyses of post-intervention performance took pre-intervention performance into account, i.e. the 'value added' by the intervention. This was done using the statistical techniques of **regression analysis** and **multi-level modelling**. Using this form of analysis it is possible to compare children's attainments at both follow-up points, after making allowance for their different starting points. In other words the statistical procedures allow us to consider progress.

3.3 Measures at pre-test and follow up

3.3.1 Reading and phonological measures

Measuring reading ability in the lower achievers in this young age group is quite difficult. Many of these children are unable to read much at all. Two standard reading tests, the British Ability Scale Word Reading test (Elliot et al, 1984) and the Neale Analysis of Reading (1988), and various other tests which assess lower-order reading skills, such as the child's knowledge of the alphabet, have been employed. The standard reading tests – one is a word recognition test (BAS Word Reading), and the other a test of prose reading with both reading accuracy and comprehension components (Neale Analysis of Reading) – are valuable for various reasons. Firstly, being standard, they offer the possibility of comparisons with broadly established norms. Secondly, their reliability and validity have been rigorously established. Thirdly, they are widely used and understood. Finally, though they may fail to be the most sensitive measures at the outset of the study, they are more suitable as the children's skills improve and it is necessary to establish baseline scores on both measures.

In her careful development of the Reading Recovery programme, Marie Clay recognised the problem of reliably identifying those children who were the poorest readers and therefore most in need of 'recovery' (Clay, 1985). Her battery of five tests, the Diagnostic Survey, which takes about 30 minutes to administer, was also used to assess lower-order reading and writing skills:

1. Letter Identification

    The child is asked to identify all upper and lower case letters. This has been found to be a powerful predictor of subsequent progress in reading of Reception year children (e.g. Tizard et al., 1988).

2. Concepts about Print

    The child's knowledge of lower-order skills, such as the fact that print contains a message, directionality of print, what is a letter and what is a word, is explored.

3. Word Test

    This is a word recognition test suitable for children with a very small reading vocabulary.

4. Written Vocabulary

    The child is simply asked to write as many words as he/she can in the space of 10 minutes. Written Vocabulary and Dictation are both measures of writing.

5. Dictation

    The child is asked to write down a short, simple, dictated passage. Incorrect spellings are acceptable as long as they show an appropriate phonic analysis, for example 'skool' instead of 'school'.

The resulting scores are referred to subsequently in this report as the Diagnostic Survey and represent the combination of all five sub-tests.[11] In addition to the Diagnostic Survey, a Book Level was established for each child, as is the Reading Recovery practice. This entailed establishing which of a series of texts, graded from 1 to 26 according to the Reading Recovery levels, children could read with 90 per cent accuracy.[12]

Phonological awareness was also assessed. Like letter identification, it is an ability measurable in pre-readers which has been found to predict subsequent reading progress. Also, the Phonological Intervention specifically targets phonological awareness and such a measure offers a direct way of identifying any intervention effects. Phonological awareness was measured at all measurement points, using the Rhyme, Initial and End Sounds Oddities Test (Kirtley et al, 1989). In this test, children are given three words, one of which is the odd one out. (In the rhyme condition it does not rhyme with the other two. In the initial sound condition, it does not start with the same letter etc.) Their task is to identify the odd one out. Children are given 10 such tasks for each of the three conditions. Scores range from 0 to 21.[13]

All of the above measures were taken at pre-test and first follow-up. At the second follow-up the Clay Diagnostic Survey and Book Level were dropped, as it was believed they would be too easy for many of the children by this stage. Instead, as a measure of spelling ability, the British Ability Scale Spelling test was used at second follow-up.

In addition, at first follow-up, a sound deletion test was used to measure phonological skill because it was less similar to the teaching format of the Phonological Intervention than the Kirtley test. A modified version of Bruce's (1964) Sound Deletion test was used to measure ability to delete sounds from spoken words. For example, childen were asked to say what word was left when the sound 'h' was taken from the front of 'hill'. Here scores range from 0 to 24. This test proved to be very difficult for the children participating in the study. Testers observed that children who were successful on the Sound Deletion test apparently reached the correct answer by mentally removing the relevant letter and reading the newly-formed word. They did not orally delete the sound to produce a new word orally without recourse to actual reading. Thus the Sound Deletion test appeared to function as a complex test of silent reading. It was felt that a slightly simpler task, that of non-word reading, would be a good alternative measure of

---

[11] Each of these tests generates a raw score and, of course, the magnitude and variance vary considerably between tests. In order to derive a total score across all the sub-tests, the raw scores were transformed so that each one had a mean of 0 and a standard deviation of 1. They were then summed and transformed again so that these total scores also had a mean of 0 and a standard deviation of 1.

[12] Level 1 texts are the simplest caption books suitable for children with very limited reading skills. Level 26 translates to a reading age of between $8\frac{1}{2}$ and $9\frac{1}{2}$ (Glynn et al, 1989, p.11).

[13] Raw scores of 3 or less in each condition are deemed poorer than chance and have been adjusted to 0. Scores of 4 or more per condition indicate increasing phonological awareness and have been adjusted to range from 1 to 7. They are then summed across the three conditions.

phonological awareness which would more closely match the children's abilities. The Snowling Non-Word Reading test was therefore substituted for the Sound Deletion test at second follow-up. In this test, children are presented with non-words of three levels of difficulty and awarded points for each word read within appropriate phonological representation.[14] As children will never have seen these words before, their ability to read them relies entirely on their ability to decode phonologically.

3.3.2 IQ measure

The children's IQs were estimated at pre-test using the BAS Short Form IQ, consisting of the following sub-tests: Naming Vocabulary, Recall of Digits, Similarities and Matrices.

3.3.3 Measure of ability with numbers

At pre-test and final post-test, the children's number skills were measured using the BAS Basic Number Skills. At pre-test forms B and C were used, at final post-test form C.

3.3.4 Training staff to administer the tests

The research team, all of whom were experienced primary teachers, were given a full training programme in the testing techniques. This involved five training days and four days practising these skills on children who would not form part of the study.

3.3.5 Measure of behaviour problems

Information on the children's behaviour was collected at pre-test and first follow-up from both teachers and parents. Both sets of respondents were asked to complete the Child Behaviour Questionnaire for Infants (Rutter, 1967). This is a widely used instrument which gives both a measure of general behaviour problems and allows for more specific analyses of particular areas of difficulty, such as over-activity or 'situational hyperactivity'.

3.3.6 Background information collected on the children

In addition to this extensive battery of tests, background information was also collected on each child: gender, age, ethnicity, take-up of free school meals both at the beginning and the end of the study, birth order, number of siblings, their number of days absent in summer terms 1992 and 1993, and whether or not English was their second language.

---

[14] There are five three-letter, one syllable words at the first level; 10 four- or five-letter, one syllable words at the second level; and 10 two-syllable words at the third level. A score of 30 was obtained by awarding 2 points for a correct answer on level 1 and 1 point for correct answers on levels 2 and 3.

3.3.7 Extra help with reading: data collected

In order to compare the cost of the different interventions with the cost of normal school provision for this group of children with reading difficulties, it was necessary to collect information on provisions made for the control group. A fuller account of the information collected appears in Chapter 8 which deals with cost effectiveness.

Details were also collected from those delivering the two interventions on the number of sessions their pupils received and over what period of time.

In addition, for each of the seven boroughs participating in the study, information was also collected on their expenditure on children with special needs. Again more details of this are available in Chapter 8.

3.3.8 The classroom/school reading environment

For every child in the study their classroom teacher in 1992/93 (the intervention year) was asked to complete a questionnaire which included a checklist of reading activities and assessment; and questions about practices in hearing children read, classroom organisation and management, classroom support for the teaching of reading and parental help. This questionnaire relied very heavily on one developed by Blatchford, Ireson and Joscelyne (1994).

CHAPTER 4

CHARACTERISTICS OF THE SAMPLE AND THE MEASURES OF READING AND PHONOLOGICAL AWARENESS

This chapter describes the children involved in the evaluation and the measures of reading used to assess the impact of the interventions.

4.1 Characteristics of the different boroughs participating in the study

The children who have taken part in the research have been drawn from seven different boroughs, each with a slightly different character. **Table 4.1** below provides demographic information on each borough both for all the Year 2 children in the selected schools and for the sub-group of poorer readers participating in the research.

Table 4.1

Schools participating in the research project by gender, take-up of free school meals and English as a second language

Boroughs (number of schools)	% of boys		% taking free school meals		% with English as a second language	
	In Yr 2	In study	In Yr 2	In study	In Yr 2	In study
Surrey (17)	49	62	15	17	6	10
Bexley (6)	46	57	11	8	3	6
Greenwich (5)	54	50	49	60	11	14
Ham.&Ful. (6)	53	64	50	56	14	16
Islington (11)	56	68	51	57	30	22
Wandsworth (11)	52	62	42	64	14	16
Westminster (7)	53	61	39	54	49	52

If the take-up of free school meals is used as an indicator of poverty, it can be seen that the children as a whole in the Surrey and Bexley schools are the least disadvantaged. In all the other boroughs more than one-third of Year 2 children were receiving free school meals. Poverty amongst those children who were involved in this evaluation, that is those with reading difficulties, was slightly more prevalent than among their Year 2 peers.

The average percentage of children taking free school meals for England as a whole was 16 per cent at the time of the study, which was about half the figure for the Year 2 children in the schools involved in the evaluation. This demonstrates the relatively high proportion of poor children in these inner-city LEAs.

The Westminster schools had a very large number of children who spoke English as their second language. These children were slightly over-represented amongst the poor readers. Boys, however, were invariably over-represented in the children selected for this study, which reflects the common finding that boys lag behind girls in reading ability.

Not only did the boroughs taking part in the study differ in terms of their demography but also, as one might expect, in the reading ability of their pupils sampled here. **Table 4.2** demonstrates this clearly.

Table 4.2

The reading ability of the entire sample of children on entry to the study, by borough

Borough (number of children)	Word Reading (% scoring above 0)	Prose Reading (% scoring above 0)	Book Level (% above Level 1)
Surrey (104)	74	39	33
Bexley (37)	89	49	59
Greenwich (30)	63	13	13
Ham.&Ful. (36)	64	8	17
Islington (71)	47	14	11
Wandsworth (68)	63	37	33
Westminster (44)	59	39	37
Total	64	28	26

Surrey was of particular interest for two reasons: it represents a contrast to the inner-city nature of most of the other boroughs; and the Reading Recovery programme in Surrey was better established than in the other participating LEAs at the time of the evaluation. For these reasons Surrey children were deliberately over-represented in the present study, making up a quarter of the sample.

4.2 Characteristics of the measures of reading and phonological awareness used

There was a good level of association between the different reading measures used, as illustrated by the size of the correlations at follow-up, given in **Table 4.3**. (Where one measure is perfectly predicted by the other, there would be a correlation of 1 and, where there is no prediction, a correlation of 0.)

Table 4.3

Correlations at first follow-up between the measures of reading and phonological awareness

	Prose Reading	Book Level	Diagnostic Survey	Phonological Awareness (Kirtley)	Sound Deletion
Word Reading	0.93	0.85	0.78	0.44	0.67
Prose Reading		0.85	0.76	0.44	0.65
Book Level			0.80	0.41	0.58
Phonological Awareness (Kirtley)					0.53

Measures of reading were not so well correlated with the two measures of phonological skill, the Kirtley oddity test and the Sound Deletion test. This is to be expected but underlines the fact that the reading and phonological measures, whilst strongly correlated, are measuring different skills. The Sound Deletion test was more closely associated with reading than the Kirtley test of phonological awareness, and both of these measures of phonological skills were only correlated at 0.53. The stronger association between reading and Sound Deletion confirms our impressions during testing that the Sound Deletion test relied heavily on the child's ability to read. The Kirtley test, in common with several other similar tests of phonological awareness, taps a range of skills, not only phonological awareness. The child must hold three words, orally presented, in short-term memory, then compare them and use phonological skills to select the 'odd one out'.

This makes demands on short-term memory, working memory and general ability to match and discriminate as well as the ability to hear sounds in words. The Kirtley test was correlated with general IQ (0.41)[1] at pre-test. The significant relationship between the Kirtley and IQ remained even after controlling for the child's reading ability.[2] In other words the Kirtley test of phonological awareness was independently related to both IQ and reading.

When children's scores on the BAS Word Reading test and the Neale Analysis of Reading were translated into reading ages, they did not agree very closely. The Neale Analysis yielded reading ages which were systematically and substantially lower than the BAS Word Reading test and were in our judgement an inaccurate reflection of the children's true level of ability. Our judgement that the Neale reading ages were inaccurate has been confirmed by other researchers.[3] For this reason we have only used the age standardised scores for the BAS test, although the raw scores on the Neale are not problematic.

The new tests introduced at the second follow-up also correlated well with the measures of reading used (Word Reading correlated at 0.87 with the BAS spelling test and at 0.74 with the Snowling test of non-word reading).

Children's performance on all the reading measures at the beginning of the study were quite good predictors of their performance nine months and 21 months later (see **Tables A3.1 and A3.2 in Appendix 3**). However, some of the tests were rather insensitive for these children with very limited reading skills. When the children were first tested, many either failed to score at all, or scored very little in the three tests which measure reading rather than pre-reading skills (as can be seen in **Table 4.2**). Even in the word reading test, where most children scored something, the median number of words read was only 2 (out of a possible 110). The Diagnostic Survey is a more sensitive measure for this ability range. For the total raw score across all the items on the Diagnostic Survey the median score was 70, which gives an indication that children could manage at least some of this test. The Diagnostic Survey was the test with the greatest predictive power and correlated with the other measures of reading at the first follow-up at around 0.64 and 12 months later, at the second follow-up, at about 0.61. The initial measure of phonological awareness, though not as powerful a predictor of subsequent reading ability as pre-test reading, showed a small but significant correlation with reading at nine months and 21 months follow-up.[4]

---

[1] The different measures of reading also showed correlations of around 0.4 with IQ.

[2] Where Kirtley at pre-test was the dependent variable and controlling for reading at pre-test in a regression analysis the effect of IQ on the Kirtley score was highly significant (B= 0.09, $p < 0.00001$).

[3] Gregory and Gregory, 1994.

[4] In the region of 0.25 and 0.3 when the children who received Reading Recovery were excluded.

The relationship between phonological awareness (as measured by the Kirtley test) and subsequent reading ability was not quite as strong in the present study as that reported by Bradley and Bryant.[5] This may well be due to the fact that our children, all selected because of their poor reading ability, showed particularly poor phonological awareness at outset. They tended to score at the very lowest levels on the initial Kirtley test with scores of around 3 out of a possible 21 (**Table 4.5**).

Table 4.4

Gender of all the children in the study, their take up of free school meals and the percentage speaking English as a second language, by experimental group

Experimental group (number of children)	% of boys	% receiving free school meals	% speaking English as a a second language
Reading Recovery Intervention children (95)	57	41	21
Within school controls (41)	66	39	10
Between school controls (157)	62	44	16
Phonological Intervention Intervention children (97)	63	42	13
Within school controls (46)	70	48	13
Between school controls (152)	61	41	15
Mean	61	42	16

---

[5] They reported correlations between sound categorisation and subsequent reading of about 0.45 in their Primary Group (Bradley & Bryant, 1985, p.51).

Table 4.5

The reading and phonological ability of children by experimental group

Experimental groups	Mean scores					
	Word Reading	Prose Reading	Book Level	Diagnostic Survey Score	Phono-logical Awareness (Kirtley)	IQ
Reading Recovery Intervention children	2	0	1	-0.3	2	91
Within school controls	4	2	2	0.4	4	96
Between school controls	6	2	2	0.2	3	96
Phonological Intervention Intervention children	3.5	1	1	-0.2	3	93
Within school controls	4.5	1.5	1	0	3	94
Between school controls	5.5	2	2	0.35	3.5	96
Total	4	1	1.5	0	3	94

4.3 Differences between the experimental groups at the beginning of the study

When the experimental groups were compared in terms of their demographic composition they were found to be very similar, although there appeared to be a tendency for children whose mother tongue was not English to be offered Reading Recovery. The percentage of children with English as a second language in Reading Recovery as a whole was very similar to that in the total sample (17 per cent as compared with 16 per cent, **Table 4.4**).

However, there were significant differences in the children's average reading abilities, amongst the experimental groups. As was to be expected from the nature of the selection procedure the Reading Recovery children were the poorest scoring group.[6] The children who attended the control schools were also slightly more advanced readers on averagethan those children attending either Reading Recovery or Phonological schools (**Table 4.5**). There is no ready explanation for this finding except that Reading Recovery may have been targeted at schools with known poor reading attainment.

The implication of this finding is that subsequent comparisons between experimental groups must take account of children's initial reading levels. Because there were differences in the average reading abilities of children at the beginning of the study, between the three groups – Reading Recovery, Phonological Intervention and Control – it would be unsatisfactory merely to compare their reading attainments at follow-up. Their performances were compared, therefore, after taking account of their initial reading abilities. This was done using a regression analysis where the Diagnostic Survey and BAS Word Reading test at pre-test was taken as the measure of initial reading ability.

4.4 Conclusion

The schools participating in the study were drawn from LEAs of different character, but they tended to have more pupils from poorer homes than the national average. The children with reading difficulties also tended to be poorer than their Year 2 peers, and boys were over-represented. The different measures of reading used correlated well with each other and were good predictors of children's subsequent reading attainment. However, the standardised tests were not sufficiently sensitive to the skills of the bottom range of readers when they entered the study at about 6 years old. The measures of phonological awareness also correlated significantly with the measures of reading but the size of the correlations was more modest as can be expected from tests designed to measure different skills. Importantly, although Reading Recovery children, Phonological children and Control children were similar in terms of age, gender and the proportion of those taking free school meals or with English as a second language they differed systematically in their initial reading ability. This means that subsequent analyses must take account of children's performance on the reading measures at pre-test.

---

[6] They were always the bottom three or four readers in their school, whereas the 'within school' control children were the next poorest readers. The children in the Phonological and Control schools were selected from the bottom six children.

CHAPTER 5

THE EFFECTS OF READING RECOVERY AND PHONOLOGICAL INTERVENTION ON CHILDREN'S PROGRESS IN READING AND THEIR PHONOLOGICAL AWARENESS

In this evaluation the heart of the matter is whether either of the interventions under examination can be demonstrated to improve children's reading in both the short and medium term.

5.1 Reading Recovery

5.1.1 How effectiveness is assessed

In order to assess the effectiveness of Reading Recovery in improving children's reading, two main sets of comparisons have been made. Reading Recovery children have been compared with other poor readers attending the same schools (the within school comparison). Reading Recovery children have also been compared with poor readers attending other schools (the between schools comparison). To take account of the differences in reading abilities that existed between these comparison groups at the outset of the study, regression analyses have been used throughout to estimate the size of the effect of Reading Recovery on reading and phonological skills. Thus we are looking at children's progress rather than their eventual levels of attainment.

The following regression statistics are presented. The B values are shown which, for each scale, estimate the number of units of progress attributable to Reading Recovery. For example, in **Table 5.1**, for the within school comparison, children who had received Reading Recovery could, on average, read eight more words on the BAS word reading test than the control children attending the same schools. In addition the effects of Reading Recovery are also presented as standard deviation units of progress.[1] In effect this standardises the results in such a way as to make comparison possible between different measures which use different scales. Thus, for example, referring again to Table 5.1, within schools, comparing the B values of the effect of Reading Recovery on Word Reading and the Diagnostic Survey, the value for Word Reading is much larger than that for the Diagnostic Survey. Once account is taken of the different scales, the units of progress attributable to Reading Recovery are, in fact, 0.69 for Word Reading and 0.93 for the Diagnostic Survey. Reading Recovery actually had a greater effect on performance in the Diagnostic Survey. An example which may give the reader a better grasp of the magnitude of effect represented by units of progress is that of IQ. An effect size of 0.75 on IQ would mean a gain of 11 IQ points on the scale, which is a medium to large effect.

---

[1] Cohen, 1977.

5.1.2 Progress in the first year (the intervention year)

The overall finding is that Reading Recovery is a very effective intervention, in the short term, for improving reading in this group of children in difficulty. For both sets of comparisons, within school and between school, Reading Recovery children made significantly more progress than the control children in every measure of reading (**Table 5.1**). The size of the Reading Recovery effects (as shown in sd units progress) are large,[2] and well worth having.

Table 5.1

The effect of Reading Recovery on reading, writing and phonological skills at first follow-up

The results of a regression analysis controlling for initial scores on the Diagnostic Survey and BAS Word Reading

	Reading Recovery comparison[3]			
Reading measures	Within schools (sample size = 64 v 40)		Between schools (89 v 153)	
	B	sd Units progress	B	sd Units progress
Word Reading	8.0	0.69 ****	9.2	0.70 ****
Prose Reading	3.2	0.41 *	5.9	0.66 ****
Book Level	6.2	0.92 ****	7.2	0.96 ****
Diagnostic Survey	0.79	0.93 ****	0.92	0.97 ****
Letter ID	2.8	0.52 *	5.0	0.71 ****
Concepts about Print	2.8	0.94 ****	2.6	0.89 ****
Word Test	2.4	0.63 ***	3.6	0.79 ****
Written Vocab.	9.6	0.54 **	11.8	0.66 ****
Dictation	6.5	1.0 ****	8.6	0.96 ****
Phonological Awareness (Kirtley)	1.3	0.25	1.2	0.24 *
Sound Deletion	2.3	0.40 *	2.9	0.56 ****

* $p < 0.05$ ** $p < 0.01$ *** $p < 0.001$ **** $p < 0.0001$

---

[2] According to Cohen's (1977) classificatory scheme.

[3] The Reading Recovery children in four schools were excluded from the within school analyses as there were no control children available in these schools.

To give a conceptually easier idea of the magnitude of progress made by the children in the course of the year we also created a sub-group of matched controls,[4] that is control children with the same initial reading ability as the Reading Recovery children. This serves the dual purpose of allowing us to compare average levels of attainment at a given time, which are more straightforward to grasp than the results of regression, and also to demonstrate that our results (shown in **Table 5.1**) hold true when children being compared are very similar before any intervention.

In the space of the eight or nine months between pre-test and first follow-up the Reading Recovery children made around 17 months' progress[5] in reading (**Table 5.2**). In the same time the control children in non-Reading Recovery schools made about nine months' progress. The Reading Recovery children had made about twice as much progress as could be expected on the basis of standardised scores, and about twice as much as the control children in non-Reading Recovery schools. The control children in the Reading Recovery schools had made more progress than the other control children, about 13 months' as opposed to nine, although less than the matched Reading Recovery children. This makes sense in the light of the fact that Reading Recovery teachers made efforts to disseminate various aspects of good practice that they had acquired in their training to the schools in which they worked. This will be discussed at greater length in Chapter 9.

Table 5.2

The effect of Reading Recovery at first follow-up: a matched controls comparison

Mean scores at first follow-up

	Reading Recovery comparison			
Reading measures	Within schools		Between schools	
	Reading Recovery (28)	Controls (32)	Reading Recovery (83)	Controls (88)
Word Reading (Reading Age)	24 (6 yrs 6 m)	16 (6 yrs 1 m)	20 (6 yrs 4 m)	9 (5 yrs 8 m)
Prose Reading	14	10	12	5
Book Level	16	9	14	5
Diagnostic Survey	0.8	0	0.5	–0.6

---

[4] Children in the matched groups were matched on the basis of their initial scores on the Diagnostic Survey.

[5] The between school matched group had an initial reading age of around 4 years 11 months (raw score 2 on the BAS), the within school matched group had a reading age around 5 years (raw score 3 on the BAS).

5.1.3 Progress in the second year (when no intervention was given)

One full school year later Reading Recovery children had still made significantly more progress in all the reading measures than control children in non-Reading Recovery schools (**Table 5.3**). The standardised effect sizes of between 0.32 and 0.42 are medium sized. However, the gap between the two groups had narrowed. The comparison between the Reading Recovery children and control children attending the same school failed to reach statistical significance at conventional levels, though the Reading Recovery children had made consistently greater progress than control children on every measure. This is partly a result of the smaller sample size of this group. Standardised effect sizes for the between school comparison of the Phonological Intervention (see **Table 5.5**) were of a similar magnitude and were statistically significant. Another possible explanation, which has already been mentioned, is that control children in Reading Recovery schools may have benefited from an improvement in classroom tuition due to dissemination of Reading Recovery principles (programme 'leakage').

Why was the effect of Reading Recovery somewhat less powerful at second follow-up? In fact this finding is consistent with the research literature reviewed in Chapter 1. It is a most difficult task to maintain children's gains after an intervention is withdrawn, and this is frequently not achieved. In the Pinnell study of Reading Recovery,[6] where children were followed up eight months after the programme had been completed (as opposed to approximately 15 months on average in the present study), there was also evidence of a reduction in the effect of Reading Recovery. The same is true of the Columbus Longitudinal study of Reading Recovery. Wasik and Slavin (1993) point out that in this study, despite the fact that the raw units between Reading Recovery and Control children remained the same across all three years the effect sizes diminished. They explain that this is a result of an interesting statistical phenomenon:

> 'The difference between these two measures (raw units and effect sizes) is that the standard deviation of the Text Reading Level (Book Level) measured increases each year, making the same raw difference a smaller proportion of the standard deviation. In more substantive terms, the size of the difference may not be diminishing (assuming the measure is an equal interval scale), but the importance of the difference is diminishing. For example, a difference of three months in a standardised reading text might be a big difference at the end of the first grade but is a small one at the end of the sixth grade.' (p. 185)

There is indeed an expectation that children coming off Reading Recovery will take time to readjust to the lack of specialised support and it is for this reason that children are frequently discontinued at a relatively high reading level to compensate for this.

On the basis of the matched control comparison, Reading Recovery children still had six

---

[6] Pinnell et al, 1994.

months' advantage in reading age over the control children in non-Reading Recovery schools at second follow-up (**Table 5.4**). The Reading Recovery children had made 25 months' progress in the space of 20 months. The control children from different schools had made 19 months' progress.

Comparing Reading Recovery children with matched Controls who attended the same schools the Reading Recovery children had made four months' more progress.

Table 5.3

The effect of Reading Recovery on reading, spelling and phonological skills at second follow-up (one full year after the intervention year)

The results of a regression analysis controlling for initial scores on the Diagnostic Survey and the BAS Word Reading test

	Reading Recovery comparison			
Measures	Within schools[7] (sample size = 66 v 33)		Between schools (91 v 151)	
	B	sd Units progress	B	sd Units progress
Word Reading	5.1	0.29	7.6	0.41 ****
Prose Accuracy	3.1	0.25	5.3	0.42 ****
Prose Comprehension	1.3	0.30	1.7	0.36 **
Spelling	1.3	0.18	2.7	0.32 **
Phonological Awareness (Kirtley)	0.3	0.01	0.1	0.03
Snowling Non-Word Reading	2.6	0.29	3.2	0.38 **

* trend, p < 0.06   ** significant at 0.01 level
*** significant at 0.001 level   **** significant at 0.0001 level

---

[7] The Reading Recovery children in five schools were excluded from the within school analyses as there were no control children available in these schools.

If the differences in raw scores shown in **Tables 5.2** and **5.4** are compared it can be seen that in this study, as in the Columbus Longitudinal Study, these differences remain much the same while their statistical significance decreases.

Table 5.4

The effect of Reading Recovery at second follow-up: a matched controls comparison

Mean scores at second follow-up

	Reading Recovery comparison			
Reading measures	Within schools		Between schools	
	Reading Recovery (29)	Controls (30)	Reading Recovery (86)	Reading (87)
Word Reading (Reading Age)	40 (7 yrs 4 m)	32 (7 yrs)	34 (7 yrs)	24 (6 yrs 6 m)
Prose Accuracy	25	19	20	13
Prose Comprehension	9	6	7	5
Spelling	21	18	18	14

5.2 Phonological Intervention

5.2.1 Progress in the first year (the intervention year)

The short-term effect of the Phonological Intervention was much more specific than that of Reading Recovery, and not as secure. The intervention had successfully improved children's performance on the test of phonological awareness which most closely matched the training given in the intervention (**Table 5.5**). However, for the within school comparison, which should be the most powerful one, there were no other significant intervention effects. Unlike the within school Reading Recovery comparison the children in Phonological schools had been randomly assigned to experimental or control condition. Also there was no attempt to disseminate the Phonological Intervention to classroom teachers, although it is possible that the profile of phonics instruction was slightly raised in participating schools. The failure of the Phonological Intervention to show any but the narrowest effects in the within school comparison puts a serious question mark against its short-term effectiveness.

Table 5.5

The effect of the Phonological Intervention on reading and writing skills at first follow-up

The results of a regression analysis controlling for initial scores
on the Diagnostic Survey and BAS Word Reading

	Phonological Intervention comparison				
Reading measures	Within schools (sample size = 91 v 44)		Between schools (91 v 108)	
	B	sd Units progress	B	sd Units progress
Word Reading	1.3	0.11	1.5	0.11
Prose Reading	1.1	0.13	0.9	0.09
Book Level	0	0	0	0
Diagnostic Survey	0.1	0.10	0.3	0.30 **
Letter ID	1.1	0.11	2.2	0.25 *
Concepts about Print	0	0	0.3	0.10
Word Test	0	0	0.6	0.12
Written Vocab.	2.2	0.10	9.7	0.50 ****
Dictation	1.6	0.17	3.1	0.42 ***
Phonological Awareness (Kirtley)	1.6	0.33 *	3.6	0.72 ****
Sound Deletion	0.8	0.17	1.5	0.34 **

* p< 0.05   ** p < 0.01   *** p < 0.001   **** p < 0.0001

In the comparison between Phonological children and children in Control schools[8] the intervention effects are much as one might predict. Phonological children, although making a bit more progress in reading than the Control children, were not significantly better off. However, the Phonological children had made significantly greater gains in the other measure of phonological skill, and on the Diagnostic Survey. The three areas of their performance which were responsible for this were letter identification, the written vocabulary test and the dictation test, which is specifically scored for phonic word analysis. As has been found by other researchers, reviewed in Chapter 1, phonic interventions seem to be particularly powerful in helping children of this age write and spell.

The results of the comparison of Phonological children with matched controls show that the Phonological children made a reading-age gain of around 10 months[9] in the space of eight or nine months from pre-test to first follow-up, as compared with the eight-month gain made by the matched children in the Control schools (**Table 5.6**). It was not necessary to match the children in the within school comparison as they had been randomly assigned within the same schools.

Table 5.6

The effect of the Phonological Intervention at first follow-up: a matched control comparison

Mean scores

	\multicolumn{4}{c}{Phonological comparison}
Reading measures	\multicolumn{2}{c}{Within schools}	\multicolumn{2}{c}{Between schools}
	Phonological children (91)	Controls (44)	Phonological children (67)	Controls (67)
Word Reading (Reading Age)	13 (5 yrs 11m)	14 (6 yrs)	14 (5 yrs 11m)	11 (5 yrs 9m)
Prose Reading	7	8	8	6
Book Level	7	8	7	7
Diagnostic Survey	–0.2	–0.1	–0.2	–0.5

---

[8] Control children from Reading Recovery schools were not included in the between schools analysis because of the ambiguity of their status. It seemed possible that they might have derived some benefit from attending a Reading Recovery school.

[9] The reading age at pre-test of the between school match was around 5 years 1 month (BAS word reading raw score = 3.4).

5.2.2 Progress in the second year (when no intervention was given)

At second follow-up comparing the Phonological children with the Control children attending the same schools (the within schools comparison) the intervention showed a positive but relatively small effect on every measure, with particular emphasis on the non-word reading and spelling. However, none of these effects reached statistical significance. In the between schools comparison, children who had received the Phonological Intervention had made significantly more progress in reading accuracy (although not in reading comprehension) and in spelling, as well as in the directly phonological skills measured. As discussed in Chapter 1, this pattern of results could be explained by the hypothesis that the Phonological Interventions are particularly powerful at improving children's spelling skills, which given time will improve their word recognition. The fact that children's reading comprehension was not significantly improved is consistent with the findings of other evaluations of primarily phonics based reading interventions. Interventions aimed at a narrower range of skills tend to have a narrower effect. The effect sizes for the between schools phonological comparisons are of a similar magnitude to the within schools Reading Recovery comparisons, but less than the between schools Reading Recovery comparisons.

Table 5.7

The effect of the Phonological Intervention on reading, spelling and phonological skills at second follow-up (one full year after the intervention year).

The results of a regression analysis controlling for initial scores on the Diagnostic Survey and the BAS Word Reading test

Reading measures	Phonological Intervention comparison				
	Within schools (86 v 44)		Between schools (86 v 105)	
	B	sd Units progress	B	sd Units progress
Word Reading	2.5	0.13	5.2	0.27 **
Prose Accuracy	1.3	0.10	2.9	0.22 *
Prose Comprehension	0.5	0.10	0.9	0.18
Spelling	1.4	0.16	2.5	0.27 *
Phonological Awareness (Kirtley)	0.1	0.02	2.4	0.49 ***
Snowling Non-Word Reading	1.5	0.18	2.8	0.33 **

* significant at 0.05 level   ** significant at 0.01 level   *** significant at 0.001 level

The evidence of the effectiveness of the Phonological Intervention is mixed. The results of the within schools comparison are not significant but some of the between schools comparisons are. The Phonological Intervention is certainly less effective than Reading Recovery and the effects narrower. To gain a better understanding of the magnitude of the difference between the Phonological and Control children we analysed the data for matched controls (presented in **Table 5.8**). The Phonological children had the same average reading age as control children attending the same schools. However, they were three months ahead of the matched controls in other schools.

Table 5.8

The effect of the Phonological Intervention at second follow-up: a matched control comparison

Mean scores

Reading measures	Phonological comparison			
	Within schools		Between schools	
	Phonological children (87)	Controls (44)	Phonological children (68)	Controls (68)
Word Reading (Reading Age)	30 (6 yrs 10m)	31 (6 yrs 10m)	32 (6 yrs 11m)	26 (6 yrs 8m)
Prose Accuracy	17	18	18	15
Prose Comprehension	6	6	6	5
Spelling	17	17	18	15

5.3 The importance of differences between schools

It is well known that children attending different schools vary systematically on many outcome measures according to which school they attend. Researchers usually refer to this as the 'school effect'. Controlling for possible sources of variance, such as academic ability on entry to the school, social class, ethnicity etc. can reduce this apparent 'school effect', but it is still necessary to be aware of its possible significance. Some schools, for example, offer a particularly high standard of education, which would produce a positive school effect. In the preceding analyses comparisons have been made between children attending different schools and it is therefore advisable to estimate the degree to which any differences in outcome are due to school effect. To this end, all preceding analyses have been repeated using multi-level modelling, a technique which estimates the contribution to individual children's scores of the particular school they attend.

For the within school comparisons, the school effect was minimal and can be disregarded. The school effect for the between schools comparisons was more substantial.[10] After taking account of this school effect, the size of the effects of the interventions remained similar to those given above in the regression analyses.[11] Some results of the multi-level modelling will be considered in the next chapter, which is concerned with the influence that factors such as social disadvantage and English as a second language have on reading progress and how they interact with the intervention. The full results of the multi-level modelling are given in Appendix 4.

5.4 Conclusion

Consistent with other research, Reading Recovery is found to be an extremely powerful method of improving children's reading and writing over a broad spectrum in the short term. Even in the longer term differences between children in the Reading Recovery programme and children in Control schools were highly significant, but the magnitude of the effect was somewhat less. Reading Recovery children also make consistently better long-term progress in reading and writing than Control children who attend Reading Recovery schools, although the differences are not statistically significant. The fact that there was a systematic effort made to disseminate various aspects of Reading Recovery practice to the classroom teachers in the Reading Recovery schools may account for this. Socially disadvantaged children benefited particularly from Reading Recovery.

The effect of the Phonological Intervention is much narrower and less powerful in the short term. In the longer term, Phonological children made greater gains than the control school children in reading as well as in phonological awareness and writing. This is consistent with our understanding of the role of phonological awareness in the development of reading as discussed in Chapter 1. In the initial stages children rely more on whole word recognition for reading but use their knowledge of phonics to write and spell. In the current study, children's use of phonics in writing strengthened their ability to analyse the sounds in words and ultimately improved their reading at second follow-up. However, the lack of any apparent intervention effects when comparing Phonological children with children attending the same schools is disappointing. These findings provide only mixed support for Bryant and Bradley's work (1985) where a very similar intervention was found to improve children's reading and spelling considerably. It is possible that the Phonological Intervention is more effective if the same number of lessons are taught over two years, as was the case in the Bryant and Bradley study, rather than over two terms as in the present research.

---

[10] The school effect on children's progress accounted for about 25 per cent of the variance on the various outcome measures.

[11] The only result where there was a difference in terms of statistical significance was for the effect of the Phonological Intervention at second follow-up. Controlling for uptake of free school meals and for English-speaking status, the intervention effect as measured by accuracy of prose reading failed to reach statistical significance at conventional levels.

CHAPTER 6

THE CONTRIBUTION OF SOCIAL FACTORS, BEHAVIOURAL PROBLEMS AND INTELLIGENCE TO READING PROGRESS AND THEIR INFLUENCE ON THE EFFECTIVENESS OF THE INTERVENTIONS

Both interventions being evaluated, but especially Reading Recovery, had significant effects on aspects of children's reading progress. However, it is of interest to see whether either intervention is especially powerful for particular children. Although the answer to this question will interest academics, it has practical significance as well. The programme could be targeted more accurately if groups of children who would particularly benefit from an intervention could be identified at the outset.

6.1 Factors which have a general effect on reading progress

In the past, various factors have been found to be associated with reading progress, in the absence of any special help with reading. In the present study we have examined the effects of some of these factors: absence from school; having English as a second language; taking free school meals; IQ; and gender. The results are presented in **Tables 6.1** and **6.2**. A regression analysis was performed, as in Chapter 5.[1] Those with the strongest effect on reading at both first and second follow-up were identified in the analyses and account taken of their influence before moving on to the next variable. All the children in the study were included in these analyses, regardless of their intervention group. By far the best predictor of reading ability was reading at the previous measurement point. However, other factors were also significant.

---

[1] **Table 6.1** presents the results of a stepwise regression, where the outcome (dependant) variable was a composite score of reading at first follow-up (N = 303). **Table 6.2** presents the results of a stepwise regression where the outcome (dependent) variable was word reading at second follow-up (N = 351). The Diagnostic Survey was used as the pre-test measure of reading. All explanatory variables were entered together.

Table 6.1

The factors predicting reading progress in the sample as a whole from pre-test to first follow-up

Predictive factors	B	Effect size (sd units)	Those making better progress
Pre-test reading	0.63	0.67 ****	Better readers at pre-test
Days absent from school	0.02	0.02 **	Those with less absence
English as a second language	0.35	0.37 **	Children with English as a second language
Free school meals	0.23	0.23 **	Children not taking free meals
IQ	0.001	tiny	No effect
Gender	0.07	0.06	No effect

* $p < 0.05$ ** $p < 0.01$ *** $p < 0.001$ **** $p < 0.0001$

Table 6.2

The factors predicting reading progress in the sample as a whole from first follow-up to second follow-up

Predictive factors	B	Effect size (sd units)	Those making better progress
Pre-test reading	1.6	0.17 *	No significant effect
Reading at 1st follow-up	14.3	1.47 ****	Better readers at first follow-up
English as a second language	−4.0	0.43 **	Children with English as a second language
Free school meals	0.32	0.03	No significant effect
IQ	0.04	tiny	No significant effect
Gender	−1.8	0.18	Boys (not significantly)

* $p < 0.05$ ** $p < 0.01$ *** $p < 0.001$ **** $p < 0.0001$

6.1.1 Poverty

In the present study children's uptake of free school meals was used as a measure of poverty. As with all social indicators, there are problems involved and this measure is a rather crude indicator. However, both poverty and uptake of free school meals have been found to be associated with reading problems in the past.[2] In most of the LEAs taking part in this study the uptake of free school meals was used as one of the factors taken into account in the allocation of money for 'additional needs' to schools; in some LEAs it was the only factor.

Our sample selected only children who were poor readers, compared with their classmates. Even within this relatively narrow range, children who took free school meals started out at the initial tests with lower scores of reading ability (**Table 6.3**).

Table 6.3

The sample as a whole, by uptake of free school meals and reading ability (on the Diagnostic Survey) at pre-test.

Reading ability	No free school meals (214)		Free school meals (156)	
	Mean	sd	Mean	sd
Mean score on the Diagnostic Survey	0.17	(0.99)	–0.22 *	(0.97)

* significantly different at 0.0001 level (t = 3.82)

As can be seen in **Table 6.1**, uptake of free school meals also predicted progress in reading in the first year. The poorer children had lower reading scores at pre-test, but even taking this into account they made less progress in their reading in this first year. In the second year of the study they held their own with the children from less disadvantaged homes.

Previous researchers have shown that poverty, overcrowding and inadequate housing are associated with poor reading attainment.[3] There are likely to be a variety of reasons for this but one factor may relate to the richness of the child's literary experience at home. One hypothesis is that many children taking free school meals may live in lone parent families where the opportunities for an adult to read to them, or hear them read, may be limited. Poverty is also likely to have an influence on the availability of books in the home.

---

[2] E.g. Barnes & Lucas, 1974; Davie et al, 1972; Yule & Rutter, 1985; Stevenson & Fredman, 1990.

[3] See Stevenson & Fredman, 1990.

It has been shown that both the number of books in the house[4] and the opportunities for a child to read to a parent[5] are significantly linked with reading ability.

6.1.2 English as a second language

Around 16 per cent of the children in the present study were not native English speakers. They were slightly disadvantaged at the outset of the study, having generally lower reading scores **(Table 6.4)**.

Table 6.4

The sample as a whole, by English speaking status and reading ability (on the Diagnostic Survey) at pre-test

Reading ability	Native English speakers (327)		Children with English as a second language (60)	
Mean score on the Diagnostic Survey	Mean 0.04	sd (1)	Mean −0.19	sd (0.94)

However, unlike the children taking free school meals, these children made better than average progress in reading in both the first and second years of the study **(Tables 6.1 and 6.2)**. Initially these children were being held back by their facility with English, but as their English improved so did their reading.

6.1.3 IQ

Children with lower IQs started the study as poorer readers.[6] Perhaps a little surprisingly, IQ score contributed little to the prediction of how much progress children made in their reading in the course of the two years of the study, once pre-test reading scores were taken into account. (IQ did predict reading attainment at first and second follow-up if pre-test reading was not controlled for.)

---

[4] Rutter, Tizard & Whitmore, 1970.

[5] Hewison & Tizard, 1980; Tizard, Schofield & Hewison, 1982.

[6] The correlation between IQ and children's reading ability at the start of the study was 0.47 ($p < 0.001$). Very similar correlations were obtained when children with English as a second language were excluded. The size of these correlations are similar to those reported by Stanovich (1986).

6.1.4 Absence from school

The number of days children were absent from school in the summer term of the intervention year had a small but significant effect on the amount of reading progress they made. This was true even after controlling for the other variables in **Table 6.1**. It is quite plausible that days missed from school would disrupt a child's learning. However, absence from school has also been found to relate to other factors such as family disruption and parental interest in education, factors which could themselves have an influence on children's learning.[7] In the present study the actual days of missed schooling would seem to be the most important factor. Absence in 1992 did not correlate very highly with absence in 1993 (0.18) and did not predict reading progress in 1993. Nor did absence in summer 1993 predict reading progress in the following year. If the effect of absence from school was due to its link with some home factor, one would expect greater stability over time.

6.1.5 Gender

Boys were over-represented in this sample of children with reading difficulties (see p. 34). However, within the selected group of poor readers there was no real difference between the boys and girls in terms of their reading ability at the beginning of the study, and gender was not significantly related to reading progress throughout the study. Although the relationship between gender and reading is well known, the actual differences typically found between boys and girls are quite small and a study of this size would be unlikely to detect them.

6.1.6 Behaviour problems

The higher prevalence of behaviour problems, both of a general nature and of a more specific hyperactive pattern, among children with reading difficulties has been consistently reported.[8] However, the reasons for this relationship are unclear. Does reading difficulty cause children to become disruptive or withdrawn, do behaviour problems impede their learning, or are both factors related to some other mediating variable such as socio-economic status or a genetic factor? Actually, the evidence points to two of these possible explanations. It would appear that in the early years reading problems are more likely to precede behaviour problems than vice versa.[9] There is also

---

[7] E.g. Wadsworth, 1979, p. 70.

[8] E.g. Rutter, 1975; Williams and McGee, 1994; Stevenson et al, 1993.

[9] McGee et al, 1988; Richman et al, 1982.

evidence to suggest that both socio-economic status[10] and a common genetic influence[11] can lead to both behaviour problems and reading difficulties.

In the present study there was evidence that the severity of behaviour problems at the beginning of the year at school was directly related to reading progress in the first year of the study, but not in the second year.[12] However, children's behaviour problems were also related to whether or not they took free school meals, their gender, and their IQ. Once these factors were included in the analysis, behaviour problems no longer had any significant effect on reading progress.[13] This is consistent with the findings of previous researchers who have commented particularly on the complex relationship between reading, behaviour problems and socio-economic status.

6.2 The characteristics of children who particularly benefit from either intervention

Having considered those factors which had an effect on the reading progress of the children in our study as a whole, we then went on to examine whether any characteristics bore a different relationship with progress for those children who had participated in one or the other of the interventions.

6.2.1 The interaction between uptake of free school meals and Reading Recovery

The only significant interaction effect identified was between Reading Recovery and uptake of free school meals.[14] At first follow-up it was clear that Reading Recovery was a more effective intervention for the children who took free school meals than for those who did not (**Table 6.5**).[15]

---

[10] Williams & McGee, 1994.

[11] Stevenson et al, 1993.

[12] A regression analysis was performed using a composite of all the reading measures at first follow-up as the dependent variable and controlling for initial reading. The effect size of behaviour problems as identified by the teacher on subsequent reading progress = 0.02, p < 0.009. There was no such relationship using either the parent measure or looking at reading progress in the second year of the study. There was also no specific effect for hyperactivity.

[13] Performing a stepwise regression analysis similar to those shown in **Tables 6.1** and **6.2**.

[14] Because several of the variables under scrutiny were associated with the schools children attended, the most suitable set of comparisons were the within school comparisons, where control children attended the same schools as the intervention children.

[15] A full account of the analysis, using multi-level modelling, is given in Appendix 4.

Table 6.5

The effects of Reading Recovery on reading progress at first follow-up, for children taking free school meals and for children not taking free school meals

Effect size

Reading measure	No free school meals (sd units)	Free school meals (sd units)
Word Reading	0.24	1.0
Prose Reading	−0.05	0.87
Book Level	0.34	1.2
Diagnostic Survey	0.34	1.0

Information on free meals was collected at pre-test and at second follow-up. At second follow-up children were classified as, either: never taking free school meals (n = 38); taking free school meals at one measurement point, either at the beginning of the study or at the end (n = 20); or as taking free dinners at both measurement points (n = 23). For the children who took free school meals throughout the study, Reading Recovery was a powerful intervention for accelerating progress in reading and spelling even one year after the end of the intervention. The size of the effects due to Reading Recovery were still large. For children who received free school meals at some time during the study, Reading Recovery was still a useful intervention, improving reading and spelling in the longer term, but the sizes of the effects were moderate. There was no evidence of any long-term intervention effects on reading for children who had never taken free school meals (**Table 6.6**). These results are of considerable interest as they suggest that Reading Recovery is a very powerful intervention for helping disadvantaged children.

Table 6.6

The effects of Reading Recovery on reading progress at second follow-up, for children taking free school meals and for children not taking free school meals

Effect size

Reading measure	Never taking free meals (sd units)	Free meals in one year (sd units)	Free meals for two years (sd units)
Word Reading	tiny	0.32	0.92
Prose Accuracy	tiny	0.33	0.77
Prose Comprehension	tiny	0.32	0.76
Spelling	tiny	0.18	0.61

What is the explanation for this interaction between poverty and the effectiveness of Reading Recovery? It is likely, as already discussed, that part of the explanation for some poor children's difficulty with reading lies in the impoverishment of their literacy environment at home and in their community. Heath[16] has described such a community in the USA, where reading was regarded as a highly functional task, engaged in only to gain essential information, and therefore unlikely to be available by any other means. Adults generally did not buy or keep books or magazines for their own reading. Children growing up in such communities are likely to be discouraged from reading much. Heath described how a child of such a community who enjoyed reading on his own was, as a consequence, viewed as peculiar.

Visiting low-income homes in San Diego, William Teale (1986) counted and timed the literacy events that occurred in the presence of each of twenty-four pre-school children. His general observation was that a relatively small amount of time was invested in these events, though there was a wide variation between homes. For example, in three of the 22 homes surveyed, children were read stories four or five times per week. However, in the other 19 homes, stories were, on average, read as little as five times per year.

Children brought up in these environments enter school with a very limited reading experience compared with their peers. It is not surprising that they may find reading difficult. Reading Recovery offers them an intensive, daily experience of reading books

---

[16] Heath, 1983.

in a carefully controlled environment which enriches them. For children from homes and communities where reading is more highly valued, but who still experience difficulties with reading, the explanations of their problems are more likely to include endogenous causes, for example, some genetic factor. It is plausible that those children will be more difficult to help, and that the widening of their reading experience for a fixed time is not sufficient to overcome their long-term problems.

6.2.2 The interaction between uptake of free school meals and the Phonological Intervention

There was no evidence of any interaction effect between the Phonological Intervention and this measure of poverty. The benefits of the Phonological Intervention were equally apparent for children who took free school meals and those who did not.

6.2.3 Other interaction effects

No other factors had an influence on the particular effectiveness of either intervention. Children's IQ did not predict the success or failure of children offered either intervention. Children for whom English was their second language made better progress on both interventions but this was also true for the control children participating in the study. Similarly, children with behaviour problems, either of a general or specifically hyperactive type, benefited from both interventions in the same way as other children in the study.

6.3 Conclusion

The most powerful predictor of children's future reading progress was their current reading ability. However, other factors also had an association with progress. Children who did not take free school meals made better progress than those who did. Children with English as a second language made a slow start but caught up with their English-speaking classmates. Good school attendance was also related to better progress in reading. In general, these same factors predicted better progress in all the groups of children participating in the study: those who received Reading Recovery or the Phonological Intervention and the control children. However, there was one exception to this. Children who were socially disadvantaged benefited particularly from being offered Reading Recovery. Children from socially disadvantaged backgrounds are more likely to have had limited experience with books before they come to school. Reading Recovery offers them the enrichment they need to develop their literacy skills. Thus Reading Recovery seems to offer the possibility of helping a section of the community in particular need.

CHAPTER 7

CHILDREN WHO FAIL TO MAKE PROGRESS ON THE INTERVENTIONS

7.1 Reading Recovery

Inevitably some children made better progress than others on Reading Recovery. Most children are judged by their Reading Recovery teachers to have made satisfactory progress and are discontinued. A smallish minority, in the present study 11 per cent, are considered to have made insufficient progress and are not discontinued. This group is discussed further in Chapter 8.

A more standardised way of looking at children who failed to progress in the present study was to select those with the poorest reading scores at first follow-up, at the end of the intervention year.[1] Children thus selected did, of course, overlap substantially with the group that was not discontinued. In **Table 7.1** these children are compared with the other Reading Recovery children who made better progress.

Of the battery of tests administered to these children the only ones which predicted lack of progress were the test of phonological awareness and the Diagnostic Survey. There was no difference between the two groups in terms of gender, English speaking, or poverty. Nor was there any difference in IQ, or any of the IQ sub-tests or in the children's ability to make visual discriminations.[2] However, even though the Diagnostic Survey is strongly associated with outcome it is still a very imperfect predictor of failure. The 12 children making poor progress at first follow-up were distributed over the bottom 50 per cent on this initial test.

---

[1] Children were selected on the basis of their scores on a composite of all the reading measures at first follow-up. Those whose secores were at least one standard deviation below the means were selected. Twelve children out of the total 89 were identitifed by this means.

[2] The Daniels and Diack test of visual discriminations was used. (1958)

Table 7.1

Reading Recovery children who failed to make good progress in the programme

Characteristics at the initial tests	Reading Recovery children (89)	
	Those who had made poor progress (12)	The rest (77)
Gender (% boys)	58%	55%
English as 2nd language (%)	17%	21%
Take free school meals (%)	42%	42%
	Mean (sd)	Mean (sd)
Vocabulary (BAS Naming Voc.)	40 (7)	43 (9)
Memory (BAS Recall of Digits)	46 (10)	43 (11)
Verbal Reasoning (BAS Similarities)	44 (6)	48 (9)
Non-verbal Reasoning (BAS Matrices)	53 (9)	51 (7)
IQ	90	90
Maths	43 (9)	45 (9)
Visual Discrimination	13 (3)	13 (3)
Phonological Awareness	1.0 (1.7)	2.5 (2.9) **
Diagnostic Survey	−0.84	0.15 ****
Letter ID	18.9	34.6 ****
Concepts about Print	10	11
Word Test	0.4	1.5 **
Writing Vocabulary	1.9	6.4 ****
Dictation	3.8	11.0 ****

7.2 Children who were non-readers at the beginning of the study

There was some concern that children with extremely limited reading ability could not make good use of either intervention. To test this we selected the children participating in the study who were complete non-readers at the initial tests.[3]

---

[3] Children scoring less than 3 on the word reading test, 0 on the prose reading test, 1 and 0 or 1 on the Book Level.

7.2.1 The benefits of Reading Recovery for non-readers

Children who received Reading Recovery were compared with control children attending other schools.[4] In **Table 7.2** the means of these two groups of children are compared. It is less important to control for initial reading ability because all the children were non-readers at the beginning of the study.

Table 7.2

The effectiveness of Reading Recovery for the sub-group who had not yet made a start with reading

Reading ability	Reading Recovery children (52) Mean (sd)	Control children attending other schools (61) Mean (sd)
1st Follow-up		
Word Reading	17 (10)	7 (7) ****
Prose Reading	10 (6)	3 (5) ****
Book Level	13 (6)	4 (5) ****
Diagnostic Survey	0.35 (0.69)	−0.92 (0.99) ****
2nd Follow-up		
Word Reading	30 (18)	20 (15) ***
Prose Accuracy	18 (11)	10 (9) ****
Prose Comprehension	6 (5)	4 (3) **
Spelling	16 (8)	12 (7) ****

** $p < 0.01$ *** $p < 0.001$ **** $p < 0.0001$

---

[4] The within school control group was too small for this analysis.

It is clear from these analyses that Reading Recovery is a highly effective intervention for children with these very limited reading skills.[5] We also looked at the effects of Reading Recovery on the progress of the other children who were slightly better readers at the beginning of the project. For these children it was more important to control for their initial reading ability and in **Table 7.3** the effects of Reading Recovery are shown for both non-readers and these slightly better initial readers. Although Reading Recovery was highly effective for both groups at first follow-up, the size of the effects were greater for those children with the most limited reading skills at the beginning of the study. At second follow-up Reading Recovery had still had a substantial effect on the progress of the initially poor readers, but only a modest effect on the initially better readers. Contrary to concern expressed in some of the schools at the outset of the study that it was not worth offering Reading Recovery to the poorest readers, this was precisely the group which benefited most.[6]

---

[5] The statistical test applied was the t-test.

[6] The picture is reminiscent of that found with free school meals in Chapter 6. In fact there is a significantly higher proportion of children taking free school dinners among the non-readers than among the readers. These different elements should be disentangled but it is not possible to do this satisfactorily in the present study.

Table 7.3

The effectiveness of Reading Recovery for children of different reading abilities

The results of a regression analysis controlling for initial score
on the Diagnostic Survey and BAS word reading[7]

| | Reading Recovery v Control children attending non-Reading Recovery schools ||||
| | Non-readers at the beginning of the study (113) || Slightly better readers at the beginning of the study (125) ||
	B	sd units progress	B	sd units progress
1st Follow-up				
Word Reading	11	1.1	6.8	0.50
Prose Reading	7.6	1.1	3.7	0.39
Book Level	9.1	1.3	5.1	0.73
Diagnostic Survey	1.3	1.2	0.47	0.76
Phonological Awareness	1.9	0.42	0.35	tiny
2nd Follow-up				
Word Reading	10.9	0.64	4	0.24
Prose Reading	7.2	0.67	3	0.24
Book Level	2.1	0.52	1.1	0.23
Diagnostic Survey	4.9	0.67	0.15	tiny
Phonological Awareness	tiny	tiny	0.14	tiny

7.2.2 The benefits of the Phonological Intervention for non-readers

It seemed possible that children could make better use of the Phonological Intervention once they had already had some experience with books and reading. The effectiveness of this intervention may well rely on children's abilities to make links between what they learn in the context of their Phonological sessions and their more general reading experience. Children with a very limited experience may find this hard to do.

---

[7] Significance values have not been reported for this analysis as we felt this could be misleading. The purpose of the table is to illustrate the differential effect of Reading Recovery in the two groups. We cannot readily determine whether there was a statistically significant interaction effect between the intervention and non-reader/reader status for technical reasons.

Table 7.4

The effectiveness of the Phonological Intervention for children who had not yet made a start with reading

Reading ability	Phonological Intervention children (52) Mean (sd)	Control children attending control schools (42) Mean (sd)
1st Follow-up		
Word Reading	7 (7)	6 (7)
Prose Reading	3 (4)	3 (5)
Book Level	3 (4)	3 (4)
Diagnostic Survey	−0.8 (1)	−1 (1)
Phonological Awareness	7 (4)	4 (4) **
2nd Follow-up		
Word Reading	20 (14)	18 (13)
Prose Accuracy	11 (10)	10 (8)
Prose Comprehension	4 (3)	4 (3)
Spelling	13 (8)	11 (6)
Phonological Awareness	9 (5)	8 (5)

** $p < 0.01$

It can be seen from **Table 7.4** that children who could not read at all at the beginning of the study did not seem to benefit from the Phonological Intervention in the same way as they did from Reading Recovery. The only area where they made significant short-term gains was in phonological awareness, but by the second follow-up this effect had faded.

Table 7.5

The effectiveness of the Phonological Intervention for children of different reading abilities

The results of a regression analysis controlling for initial score on the Diagnostic Survey and BAS word reading.

	Phonological v. Control children attending Control schools			
	Non-readers at the beginning of the study (93)		Slightly better readers at the beginning of the study (106)	
	B	sd units progress	B	sd units progress
1st Follow-up				
Word Reading	1.8	0.25	1.2	0.09
Prose Reading	0.9	0.19	1.0	0.10
Book Level	0.4	tiny	0.1	tiny
Diagnostic Survey	0.36	0.26	0.30	0.49
Phonological Awareness	2.7	0.26	4.6	0.90
2nd Follow-up				
Word Reading	3.9	0.28	6.1	0.36
Prose Accuracy	2.2	0.24	3.1	0.25
Prose Comprehension	0.2	tiny	1.5	0.31
Spelling	3.6	0.50	1.0	0.12
Phonological Awareness	1.6	0.33	3.3	0.75

For a more precise picture of the differential effectiveness of the Phonological Intervention we compared the size of the intervention effects for the two groups of children, those who were non-readers at the beginning of the study and those who had at least some rudimentary reading skill at the outset (**Table 7.5**). Using this more precise form of analysis the Phonological Intervention did have a significant, though modest, effect on the initial non-readers' ability to tackle the Diagnostic Survey at first follow-up, and there was a significant effect on spelling apparent at second follow-up. However, the intervention effects tended to be smaller (though not invariably) for those children who were non-readers at the outset of the study.

7.3 Conclusion

The only factors which predicted very low reading attainment after the children had been taught on the Reading Recovery programme were initial reading or pre-reading skills and phonological awareness. Neither IQ nor visual discrimination nor any of the social variables predicted these very poor reading outcomes. Even poor initial reading levels were by no means accurate predictors of a poor outcome. Many children who made a poor start in reading made good progress. In fact, Reading Recovery was particularly effective for the children with the most limited reading ability at the outset of the study (roughly half the sample).

CHAPTER 8

THE COST EFFECTIVENESS OF READING RECOVERY AS COMPARED WITH OTHER FORMS OF READING SUPPORT

The cost of Reading Recovery has always been a matter of concern. It is an intensive intervention and demands a year's in-service training for each Reading Recovery teacher. However, it would be mistaken to assume that children eligible to receive Reading Recovery are otherwise inexpensive to educate. These children in the bottom 20 per cent of readers are usually offered other forms of specialised help in the absence of Reading Recovery.

8.1 Specialised reading help at school level

8.1.1 Amount of specialised reading help given

Information was collected on the specialised reading help given to every child in the present study. The researchers asked each child's class teacher if the child was given any help with reading by a *teacher other than themselves* during the school years 1992/93 and 1993/94.[1] In addition, at the end of 1993/94, it was established whether or not a child had received, or was in the process of receiving, a Statement of Special Educational Needs. The number of minutes of specialised help per week given to each child, averaged over the school year, was calculated from the information collected from class teachers.[2]

Reading Recovery teachers gave details of the number of Reading Recovery sessions given to each child receiving that intervention, over how many weeks, the number of sessions missed through child absence and the outcome (ie successfully discontinued, not discontinued from the programme). The average length of time spent in Reading Recovery was 21 weeks, during which time children received an average of 77 sessions. Each session was of 30 minutes duration. Over a 39 week school year, children thus received an average of 59 minutes Reading Recovery weekly. Reading Recovery teachers

---

[1] This information was collected at the end of the school year 1992/93 (the intervention year) and again at the end of the school year 1993/94. Teachers were asked if specialised help was given during the autumn, spring or summer term; whether this was in a group or in an individual setting; for how many minutes weekly; and for how many weeks per term.

[2] Where the help was given in an individual setting this information is directly comparable with both the Reading Recovery and the Phonological Intervention. However, where children were seen in a group, the actual cost of the minutes of individual help received by each child was calculated as a fraction of the teacher's time with the group. In order to make a comparison of costs across the different groups of children, the amount of time in a group setting was divided by the number of children in the group. This gave an estimate of the proportion of the teacher's time devoted to a particular child. The total amount of individual and group help (thus calculated) given over the course of the year was then summed and expressed as the average number of minutes help given weekly. For the year 1992/93 no information on group size was systematically collected. It was assumed that the average group size was five children which seemed a reasonable estimate of the range, normally between four and six. The mean group size for the year 1993/94 was five.

were also asked to give details of all the children they saw in the course of the school year 1992/93, not only those children participating in the research. The teachers also reported how many hours they worked on Reading Recovery weekly and how much they were paid for this work. The average time devoted to Reading Recovery weekly by the 22 teachers involved was 10½ hours and an average of 10 children per teacher completed the programme in the course of the year.[3] Each child received an average 63 minutes weekly of Reading Recovery, averaged over the year, confirming the figure arrived at by a slightly different means and on the basis of the children participating in the study alone.

Children in the Phonological group received 40 10-minute sessions, making an average of approximately 10 minutes weekly over a 39 week year.

Table 8.1 shows the amount of specialised reading help minutes expressed as a mean number of minutes given to children in the two years during which this was monitored.

Table 8.1

Specialised reading help 1992/93 and 1993/94

School/ Experimental condition	92/93 Minutes per week, excluding the intervention	92/93 Minutes per week provided in one-to-one intervention	92/93 Total specialised help	93/94 Minutes specialised help per week	92-94 Average weekly specialised help over two years
Read Rec. Schools RR children Con. children	3 mins 9 mins	59 mins –	62 mins 9 mins	10 mins 10 mins	36 mins 9.5 mins
Phonological schools Phon children Con children	12 mins 7 mins	10 mins –	22 mins 7 mins	17 mins 20 mins	19.5 mins 13.5 mins
Control schools	21 mins		21 mins	22 mins	21.5 mins

A number of interesting findings emerge from this table. The most important in view of the costs is that children in Control schools received considerable amounts of specialised help with reading. In the intervention year they received a weekly average of 21 minutes

---

[3] If children had half or a quarter of their programme in 1992/93 and the rest in the preceding or following year, they would be counted as for the appropriate fraction (0.5 or 0.25).

help, one third the amount received by Reading Recovery children. In the second year children in the Control schools received twice as much help as the Reading Recovery group. Over the course of the two years, children in the Control schools received 60 per cent of the time given to the Reading Recovery children in the form of specialised help.

Control children in the Intervention schools receive less specialised help in the intervention year than children in Control schools. This suggests that specialised help operates at class or school level, rather than at the level of the individual. It is to be expected in the Reading Recovery schools that specialised help should be concentrated in the Reading Recovery programme. In the Phonological schools we know that the amounts of specialised help available at school level were similar to those in Control schools. It is plausible that since intervention was being offered from outside to some needy children in Year 2 the specialised help made available by the school was re-allocated to other year groups. Further support for this is provided by information collected in 1993/94. Poor readers in Reading Recovery schools, where a substantial amount of the special needs budget is being spent on Reading Recovery, receive less specialised reading help than children in the other schools. Children in Phonological schools, where the intervention was not paid for from the school budget, receive about the same amount of help as children in Control schools, probably because the intervention had ceased. The minutes of specialised help in the Control schools stays very constant.

Considering the availability of specialised help as a feature of school organisation rather than as a reaction to individual children's learning problems is supported by the multi-level modelling analyses, discussed later in the chapter. It is, however, worth remarking that there was a very large variation between different schools in the amount of specialised help offered, as is illustrated below. **Figure 8.1(a)** shows the amount of specialised reading help available for children with special needs in the Phonological and Control schools and **Figure 8.1 (b)** shows the amount of specialised reading help given to those children in Phonological and Control schools participating in this study in 1993/94.

The extent to which children are offered specialised help is a poor measure of either individual need or level of reading ability because it is heavily influenced by the availability of resources.

Confirmation of the accuracy of these estimates of specialised help was calculated from other information collected. Headteachers in all the study schools were asked in June 1993 how much specialised staff time was allocated to reading support in their school and what proportion of this support was for the bottom 20 per cent of readers. On the basis of this information, the minutes of additional help with reading available weekly for each child in the bottom 20 per cent of children on roll was calculated for the control schools.[4]

---

[4] Complete information was received from 16 of the 18 Control schools. It was assumed that no additional help was given in the reception classes. This seemed a justifiable assumption on the basis of the headteachers' response to a question concerning the age at which their pupils were considered for specialised reading help.

Headteachers reported that these children received an average of 21 minutes additional reading help, exactly the same figure arrived at by asking their class teachers. To the extent that children remain within the bottom 20 per cent of readers, they can expect this level of provision *throughout* their primary school career.[5]

Table 8.1 (a)

Minutes of specialised reading help for each child in the bottom 20% of readers in the Phonological and Control schools

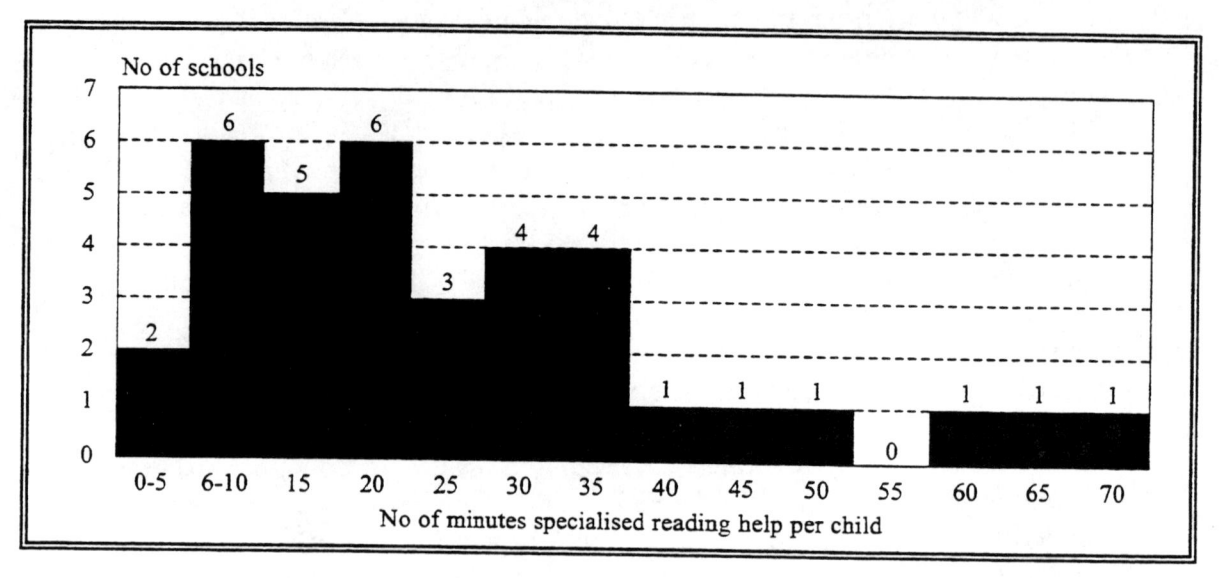

Table 8.1 (b)

Minutes of specialised reading help in 1993/94 given to the children from the Phonological and Control schools participating in the study

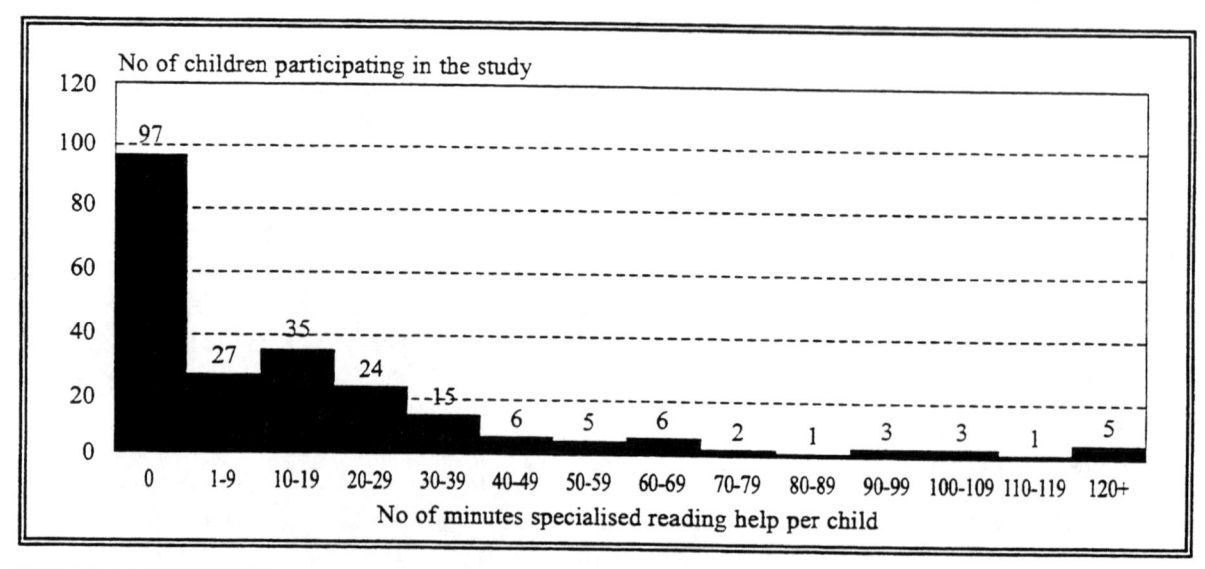

---

[5] Again, a very large variation between schools in the amount of reading support available was apparent.

8.1.2 The cost of additional reading tuition: the teacher

The cost in terms of a teacher's time for taking one child through Reading Recovery would be approximately £1,000.[6] If supply teacher rates of pay were used the figure would be lower, around £780 per year.[7]

The cost per child for teaching time only for the Phonological Intervention was £354.[8] The cost for the teacher's time required to give the control children 21 minutes individual help weekly would be in the region of £280.[9]

Table 8.2 shows that the most expensive intervention per child is the Reading Recovery Intervention. However, the most expensive intervention in terms of cost per hour is the Phonological Intervention. The fact that the researchers were operating as peripatetic teachers accounts for some of the expense. This should underline the fact that remedial help which is not available from a member of school staff is always expensive. Reading Recovery is more expensive because each child is given more minutes of help.

Table 8.2

Cost of specialised reading tuition (teacher time only)

Type of tuition	Average cost of tuition per child during the intervention year	Minutes tuition weekly	Cost of tuition if given for one hour weekly	Average cost of specialised tuition over two years (1992-94)
Reading Recovery children	£780-£1,000	59	£780-£1,000	£1,030
Phonological children	£354	10	£2,124	£581
Control children in Control schools	£280	21	£840	£573

---

[6] The Reading Recovery teacher's reported average salary was roughly £1,000 per annum for each hour worked per week. This figure, which was for 1992/93, does not include on-costs, National Insurance costs or superannuation.

[7] Estimating £100 per diem, for 5 working hours, the cost of 1 hour per week for 39 weeks = £780.

[8] This was the actual cost of teaching the children based on the research officer's salary (ie £17,000 pa including London weighting). This figure did not include training, travelling, supervision etc.

[9] Assuming an annual salary of £20,000 (including London weighting where applicable, but not National Insurance or superannuation).

None of the additional costs of such items as training, travelling, supervision are included here. To consider which intervention was the most expensive in terms of value for money, that is in terms of progress in reading achieved for the money spent, it is necessary to examine the effectiveness of the interventions.

8.1.3 Effectiveness of specialised help

Comparing Reading Recovery children with those in the Control schools, the Reading Recovery group made 25 months progress in their reading age over a 20 month interval as compared with the 19 months progress in the Control group. Thus Reading Recovery children made five months 'more progress' than might be expected on the basis of the standardised test scores in the time involved. Control children made a month less progress in reading age than might be expected on the basis of standardised test scores despite the additional 21.5 minutes weekly specialised individual help over the two year period.

It is also possible to examine more accurately whether the amount of help given to Control children bore any relationship to the progress they made in their reading.[10] For each school year separately, progress in reading was compared against the amount of specialised reading help the children received.[11] There was no evidence that the amount of specialised help (number of minutes) in either year was significantly related to children's reading progress.

Results of the analyses using multi-level modelling, which compare within and between school variation, suggest that specialised help with reading operates at school level rather than at pupil level and might, therefore, be standing for some other aspect of school organisation, such as a particular attention to special needs, or reading.

For the two year period covered by the evaluation, each Reading Recovery child cost approximately £1,030 (£890 in the first year and £140 in the second year) in extra teacher time. For the same period, the children who received the Phonological intervention cost an estimated £581 and the children in Control schools cost £573. We could measure no gain in reading that could be attributed to the expenditure of the £573 per Control child, using either their gain in reading age as compared with the standardised scores, nor any

---

[10] When examining the effectiveness of amount of help it was not clear whether or not the minutes of help given in a group setting should be taken as a whole or whether group size should be accounted for. Specialised help was therefore calculated both for the total number of minutes spent in a group and for this figure divided by group size. Results reported below, using both techniques, were similar.

[11] As before, regression analyses were run on the 185 Control children for whom complete data were available. For 1992/93, the outcome (dependent) variable was a composite of all the reading measures at first follow-up (a Z score). The regression term was calculated after entering pre-test reading scores and average minutes weekly specialised reading help. The effect of specialised help was tiny. The analysis was repeated for 1993/94 using Word Reading at second follow-up as the outcome (dependent) variable and entering the reading score at first follow-up and the average minutes of specialised help for 1993/94. Again, the specialised help effect was tiny.

extra gain for larger amounts of specialised help. This is not to say that children in the Control group did not benefit from specialised tuition: some may have made additional gains, some may have fallen back. Although specialised help differed greatly from school to school, the composite picture is not encouraging. Our findings are consistent with other research discussed in Chapter 1. A recent evaluation of remedial programmes in the USA[12] found that many tended to be rather narrow in their focus (described by the authors as 'skill-and-drill') and also to result in actual loss of total reading instruction time for the children involved. The children who were withdrawn were missing classroom reading instruction. A recent UK report by the Audit Commission[13] commented on the quality of the learning experience offered by some special needs teachers in primary schools that lessons often lacked pace, that there was a lack of assessment, and in some cases there was a low level of pupil expectation.

It is not sufficient to offer children specialised help: that help must be of a high standard. It could be argued on the basis of this evaluation that the specialised help given to the Control children was, in fact, the most expensive, compared with Reading Recovery and the Phonological Intervention, in terms of value for money.

The Phonological Intervention cost little more than the normal provision for these poor readers, but the Phonological children's reading and spelling were significantly better than that of the Control children in the Control schools.

The most expensive Intervention was Reading Recovery but it was also the most effective; it had a broad effect on children's reading and spelling even at the end of the second year. Also, the level of special provision for Reading Recovery children in the year following the intervention was half of that in Phonological or Control schools. Our data suggest that Control children will continue to receive substantial amounts of specialised tuition throughout their primary school. It is quite possible that in a few years Reading Recovery would become less expensive than other special needs provision when calculated over a child's school career. American research suggests that Reading Recovery leads to gains that are maintained[14] and that investing in it saves money later on in other aspects of the budget.[15] Also, from the research reviewed in Chapter 1, it appears that improving children's reading will benefit the child in a broad range of developmental and academic outcomes later in life.

---

[12] Allington & McGill-Franzen, 1990.

[13] Audit Commission, 1992.

[14] Pinnell et al, *The Columbus Longitudinal Study,* 1988. A further year's worth of data is reported in Reading Recovery Program, 1991.

[15] Dyer, 1992.

8.1.4 The length of the Reading Recovery programme

For an intensive intervention such as Reading Recovery the time taken to put a child through the programme has considerable bearing on the costs. The maximum recommended programme length for Reading Recovery is between 20 and 26 weeks. It is rather worrying, therefore, that *on average* the children in this study received 21 weeks of Reading Recovery. This may in part have been due to the fact that many of the teachers, although fully trained, were only in their first post-training year. In Surrey, the borough with the most established programme, average programme length was 18 weeks (67 sessions) although still not the 14 week average reported by Clay in New Zealand in the field trials of much better readers.

As was seen in Chapter 4, Surrey children had slightly higher levels of reading than children from some of the other boroughs. This offers another potential explanation for the shorter programme length in Surrey. Glynn and his colleagues (1989) have reported that the poorer children's reading ability on entry to Reading Recovery, the longer they tend to take in the programme. We also found that initial reading ability was a strong predictor with the number of weeks a child received Reading Recovery.[16] Children who were non-readers[17] on entry to the study took an average of 24 weeks (and 88 sessions) to complete the programme.

However, when we controlled for initial reading scores, children in Surrey still completed the programme more quickly than children in other LEAs.[18] Thus there is reason to be optimistic that programme length and thus programme costs should decrease as Reading Recovery becomes established in an LEA. The cost of sending one child through Reading Recovery in Surrey in the year 1992/93 was approximately £763, in terms of teacher's salary, compared to an average of roughly £932 in the other boroughs.

8.2 Reading Recovery: discontinuation

As children take part in Reading Recovery a judgment is made as to whether they have progressed satisfactorily to benefit from 'normal classroom reading' instruction. When progress is judged to be have been satisfactory, children are 'discontinued'. It would improve the cost effectiveness if it were possible to identify children at the outset who would not make progress in the programme, especially bearing in mind that these problematic children take much teacher time. Of the 89 children who received Reading Recovery in the present study five children did not complete the programme fully because

---

[16] Correlation = -0.35, $p < 0.001$, $n = 89$.

[17] See Chapter 7.

[18] We used a regression analysis, where programme length was the dependent variable to compare Surrey with all the other boroughs, controlling for initial reading. B = 4.2. Sd Units Progress = 0.65, a largish LEA effect on programme length.

the children changed school.[19] Of the remaining 84, 89 per cent were discontinued and 11 per cent were considered to have made insufficient progress and, therefore, still gave cause for concern. The nine children who failed to make adequate progress received an average of 25 weeks tuition, and at the end of this time were still judged to be poor readers. At pre-test, these children certainly had lower than average scores on the Diagnostic Survey. However, it would have been necessary to reject the bottom 42 per cent of the Reading Recovery children in the study to ensure that none of the programme's 'failures' were given the intervention. The children's IQ scores did not improve accuracy of predicting which children would fail. Thus a small percentage of failures seems inevitable. Also, even though children failed to reach a sufficient standard for discontinuation this does not mean that they gained nothing from the programme. It is very likely that they have deep-seated problems related to reading. However, it may prove possible to identify these children at an earlier stage in the intervention, perhaps withdrawing the programme after 20 weeks for children who have made very little progress. Clearly it is unwise to offer a preventative programme of upwards of 25 weeks to children who fail to respond satisfactorily.

8.3 Children with statements of special educational needs

The most expensive form of special needs provision in the UK is offered to children with a Statement of Special Educational Needs. The government recommends this for approximately 2 in 100 children. For a child who is given support of this kind the cost of teacher help for one hour weekly is typically around £1,000; for support from an ancillary the price is much less, around £200. However, these children normally receive substantially more than one hour per week. In Surrey, where precise figures were made available to us, the average number of hours per week of teacher support was between two and a half and three hours, and for ancillary staff the average figure was seven hours weekly. Once a child receives a statement, it tends to continue until the end of his or her school career.

It was therefore of interest to establish how many of the children in the present study had received statements, and if so whether the reading interventions had any effect on this. The problem with using service provision as a measure of need has already been discussed. Provision is dependent on many things. For example, it is clear both from our own study and also from that of Glynn and his colleagues (1989) that some children who were offered Reading Recovery in one school would be considered quite good readers in another school. In a special needs audit carried out in one of the boroughs in our study, the auditors suggested that where schools received small or insufficient allocations for special needs through their delegated budget 'this increases the pressure on schools to press for statement funds'. In other words some schools would feel that they needed money through statements to support their general special needs provision. During our own work in schools it was not uncommon to hear teachers refer to the fact that a statement for 'Johnny' was very useful because it also allowed 'Kate' and 'Riad' to receive some additional support into the bargain.

---

[19] These children all received at least 20 weeks Reading Recovery tuition.

Marie Clay suggests that Reading Recovery aids early identification of intractable reading problems because of its procedures for referring children on if they fail to make satisfactory progress. She suggests that the demand for remedial special needs support may actually increase in the early years due to more precise assessment. Thus a clearly defined school-based intervention should make processing a statement more efficient in the English system because the procedures require evidence of a school's efforts to overcome a child's difficulties before a statement can proceed under the Code of Practice (1994).

With this background, we looked at statementing for the children in our study.

Table 8.3

Statements of children in the study

	Children in the process of statementing in July 1994	Children who had received a statement in July 1994
Reading Recovery children (92)	9 (10%)	2 (2%)
Phonological children (87)	6 (7%)	3 (3%)
Control children (187)	17 (9%)	4 (2%)

Table 8.3 shows no difference between the three groups of children, Reading Recovery, Phonological or Control, in either the proportion of children in the process of statementing or the proportion who had received statements.

8.4 Teacher training costs

The cost of training a teacher in Reading Recovery is approximately £1,000[20] for the year, to set the teacher up with the appropriate equipment, including books for the school (estimated at £350), and to pay a proportion of the tutor's salary (estimated at £750[21]). This does not include the teacher's time, about half a day a week, as he or she will be teaching children during this time.[22]

---

[20] These figures were kindly supplied by Angela Hobsbaum at the Institute of Education.

[21] A tutor's annual salary including NIC's and superannuation was approximately £30,000 in 1992/93. About half of their time is spent teaching Reading Recovery to children. About one fifth of their time can be spent on duties other than training, leaving 0.3 of their time for training approximately 12 teachers.

[22] Though a teacher in training is less cost-effective during the training year.

The cost of training a teacher in the Phonological Intervention was approximately £300, including supplying the teacher with the appropriate equipment.[23]

It was not possible to make an estimate of the cost of training the teachers who gave the Control children specialised help.

Keeping in mind the importance of considering cost in relation to benefit, the teacher training costs should be considered in the light of the research evidence reviewed in Chapter 1. Research has shown that children taught by specially trained, well motivated teachers make more progress. If an intervention is quite intensive, and therefore relatively costly to deliver, it makes sense to invest money in training to maximise the programme's effect.

8.5   Management at LEA level

Where a programme is being offered in a number of schools some form of management across schools is necessary. As described in Chapter 2 the Reading Recovery Intervention includes in its design a self-sufficient system of teacher training and monitoring.

It has not been possible in the current research to examine all the aspects of the implementation of Reading Recovery. It has certainly not been possible to consider the issue of 'programme drift', in other words how authentically either Reading Recovery or the Phonological Intervention would be taught several years after training. Yet if the content and mode of delivery of these interventions are relevant to their effectiveness, and the evidence suggests that they are,[24] then programme drift has the potential to undermine their value. It is worth stressing this point as it is frequently overlooked. No matter how good an intervention is, if it is taught badly, and imprecisely, it can be worthless. The quality of implementation is extremely important.

The person with the main responsibility for the management of Reading Recovery at LEA level is the Reading Recovery Tutor. The annual cost of the tutor, excluding that part of his or her salary already costed under teacher training, was roughly £21,000.[25] For a substantial proportion of this time the tutor teaches children,[26] and can therefore be regarded as part of the LEA central special needs provision. The remaining part of the tutor's time is spent on a wide range of activities including maintaining the integrity of Reading Recovery teaching. They support trained Reading Recovery teachers, monitor selection of children and their graduation from the programme, monitor the costs and

---

[23] As in the case of Reading Recovery, the cost of the trainee teachers' time is not included.

[24] Especially Pinnell et al, 1994.

[25] Including NIC's and superannuation.

[26] Two hours to two and a half hours per day: usually, this would take up the tutor's mornings.

delivery of the programme more generally and also provide a wide range of INSET, beyond the direct teaching of Reading Recovery. The effects of this could be detected in various ways in the Reading Recovery schools participating in this study, as outlined in Chapter 9. INSET training is also provided to schools not currently running Reading Recovery. The annual cost to the LEA of running Reading Recovery including the entire cost of the Reading Recovery tutor, ongoing professional development and management of the programme (ie including the teacher training aspect of the tutor, already estimated under teacher training) is in the region of £35,900.[27]

There is no equivalent figure for the Phonological Intervention. The amount of money spent on managing the needs of a similar group of children, not being offered Reading Recovery, is extremely difficult to estimate. In the absence of virtually any published material we gathered information on spending on pupils with special educational needs from each of the LEAs in our study. However, the cost of management was usually unavailable. For three LEAs, where figures were obtained, the costs of those serving some of the same functions as Reading Recovery tutors were roughly £658,000, £628,000 and £429,200 respectively.[28] These figures represent expenditure for children with special needs across the whole school age range. Estimates of expenditure for Year 2 children only are roughly £60,000, £57,000 and £39,000.[29] Not all children with special needs may have literacy problems. However, it was clear from the survey of special needs provision in primary school carried out by Gipps and her colleagues (1987) that the vast majority of that provision related to tuition in some aspect of literacy. For example, in one of the LEAs in the present study it was estimated that about 85 per cent of the children in mainstream schools who had Statements of Special Educational Need had 'more or less a combination of general or specific learning difficulties sometimes with associated emotional or behavioural difficulties'.

Lack of clarity, lack of monitoring and lack of accountability in special educational needs (SEN) provision have been specifically identified as problems, both locally and nationally. Programmes, such as Reading Recovery, which precisely define their target population and make provision for monitoring and controlling the expenditure of resources, offer some solutions to these problems, but at a cost. It may also be wise to consider the cost of insufficient management and control; an excerpt from a recent audit of provision for children with special educational needs in one LEA illustrates this point:

> 'The audit identified evidence of weaknesses in the area of management and administration: no monitoring of the £3 million funding delegated to schools in

---

[27] We are indebted to Angela Hobsbaum of the Institute of Education for helping us make this estimate.

[28] This included LEA special needs section staff, Educational Psychologists and Inspection/advice on SEN.

[29] Assuming the total represented the cost of children from Year 1 to Year 11 we divided the totals by 11 to make an estimate for 1 year.

1992/93 and no guidelines for schools on how it should be used; poor historical cost-control and budgeting for special schools, units and recoupment, resulting in excessively expensive unit places (in the case of three day units, places currently cost up to £26,000 per child) and no invoicing for the estimated £4.6 million owed to the borough as recoupment income; inadequate arrangements for monitoring annual reviews of individual pupils' statements.'[30]

The following recommendation concerning management was made by the Audit Commission:

'LEAs should ensure that they are able to monitor whether the level of resources for pupils in ordinary schools continues to be appropriate. To achieve this, the LEA should delegate the task to a level where the officer has a sufficiently narrow range of responsibilities to enable him or her to monitor individual pupils.'

Reading Recovery provision at LEA level is very much in line with these recommendations for effective practice.

8.6 Conclusion

The cost of specialised help given to children on the Reading Recovery programme was considerably more than that spent on either the Phonological or the Control children. In fact the Phonological Intervention was only marginally more expensive than the specialised help available in the Control schools. However, the cost gap between Reading Recovery and the other interventions had already narrowed between first and second follow-up, and it seemed likely that it would narrow further. This was due to the fact that a substantial amount of specialised help was offered to these Control children with reading difficulties and it was offered in each year of the study, whereas the cost of Reading Recovery was concentrated in the intervention year. Also there is some evidence that the cost of Reading Recovery drops as teachers become more efficient in its use. Most of the teachers whose children have been evaluated in the present study were in their first post-training year. It is not possible to look at long term cost benefits at this stage but there are considerable long term costs associated with illiteracy.[31]

In terms of value for money it seems fairly clear that the specialised help offered in the Control schools was the least cost-effective. For a marginally greater cost the Phonological Intervention offered a significantly greater improvement in reading and spelling. The cost of Reading Recovery was substantially more in the short term, but then so was pupil progress. The costs of all forms of specialised help go beyond the school based cost of the teacher as training, management and monitoring are invariably involved.

---

[30] LEA Audit of provision for children with Special Educational Needs, October 1993 and Audit Commission, 1992.

[31] See, for example, the discussion in Chapter 1.

Unfortunately, although these costs are fairly clear for Reading Recovery they are not readily available for the other two conditions, beyond the initial training cost of the Phonological Intervention. Much of the ongoing expense associated with Reading Recovery at LEA level is probably an essential aspect of any well run special needs section.

CHAPTER 9

THE SCHOOL ENVIRONMENT

The precise nature of the school and classroom environment has considerable influence on what children learn.[1] In the present study there was no systematic attempt to influence classroom practice as the interventions were taught outside the classroom. However, Reading Recovery tutors from the seven LEAs participating in this evaluation consistently reported that they gave INSET training on various aspects of Reading Recovery to all the staff in Reading Recovery schools.[2] In addition, the Reading Recovery teachers were members of the school staff and as such might be expected to have some influence on school reading policy and practice. In the present context, it is important to examine any systematic differences in the classroom approach to the teaching of reading between Reading Recovery schools, Phonological schools and Control schools. The effectiveness of both the interventions being evaluated have in part been assessed by comparing Intervention children with Control children in the same schools. If the intervention affects not only the experimental children but also, in a diluted form, the Control children the effects of a within school comparison will understate the power of the intervention.

9.1 The classroom environment: information collected

As described briefly in Chapter 3 all the class teachers of children participating in the study were asked to give details about aspects of the way they taught reading, including: methods of assessment used; the amount of time they heard children reading; the use of reading schemes; and the grading of non-scheme books. In addition, they were asked to complete a checklist of 49 reading activities identifying which they had taught in the last week.

To gain the class teacher's own impressions of the way in which the different interventions had affected them, teachers in Reading Recovery and Phonological schools were also asked the extent to which they felt the intervention in their schools altered the way they taught reading in the classroom.

9.2 Reading Recovery

9.2.1 The effect of Reading Recovery on the teaching of reading in the classroom

Out of the 47 classroom teachers in the Reading Recovery schools, 43 returned their

---

[1] Eg Adams, 1990; Mortimore et al, 1988; Tizard et al, 1988.

[2] Training was given, in particular, in the area of assessment and the use of running records, a technique of monitoring children's reading similar to miscue analysis.

questionnaires. Of these, 84 per cent believed that Reading Recovery had altered the way they taught reading in the classroom, and 9 per cent reported that it had changed their classroom teaching substantially.

Analysis of the questionnaires showed that in many ways the classroom teachers in Reading Recovery schools use similar strategies to the teachers in the other schools.[3] There was, for example, no difference in the number of reading activities that they had taught over the last week. On average, classroom teachers in Reading Recovery schools had taught 20 activities in the past week, in the Phonological schools they had taught 19 activities on average, and in the Control schools 17, from a menu of 49 on the questionnaire. An exploratory cluster analysis was performed on the reading activities data. Activities tended to cluster into those taught by most teachers, those taught by about 50 per cent of teachers and those that were used by relatively few. However, there was no systematic difference between types of schools using these clusters. Similarly, in looking at much of the teachers' description of the classroom reading environment, although practices varied between schools, they often did not vary significantly by school type (Reading Recovery, Phonological or Control). For example, 82 per cent of the Reading Recovery school classroom teachers reported that time was set aside for silent reading, as did 65 per cent of the Phonological school classroom teachers and 78 per cent of the Control school teachers.[4] In 74 per cent of Reading Recovery school classes all children were sent home with books every week, in Phonological schools 62 per cent and in Control schools 61 per cent. Teachers were asked how many minutes weekly they listened to children read. They were specifically asked to answer this question (and those concerning the reading activities) for the readers in the bottom 20 per cent of the reading ability in their class, as there was evidence from the study by Blatchford and his colleagues (1994) that teachers differentiated their practice in the light of the pupils' ability. Teachers in the three types of school (Reading Recovery, Phonological and Control) estimated that they listened weekly to each pupil reading for 26 minutes, 27 minutes and 24 minutes respectively. This is almost certainly an exaggeration since from observation of infant classrooms, Tizard et al (1988) estimated the norm was around eight minutes weekly per child, a level recently confirmed by Plewis and Veldman (1995). Even allowing for the fact that teachers are likely to listen more frequently to their poor readers,[5] the gap between times reported here and those reported by Tizard and her colleagues are too great to be explained by the difference in reading ability of the pupils sampled.

---

[3] 28 teachers out of 44 from the Phonological schools returned their questionnaires and 20 teachers out of 36 from the Control schools.

[4] The figure reported in the study by Ireson et al, 1994, was 87 per cent.

[5] Ireson et al, 1994

However, in some important ways (consistent with the nature of Reading Recovery) class teachers in Reading Recovery schools differed in their practice from their colleagues (**Table 9.1**). They reported using running records as a method of assessment significantly[6] more often than their colleagues (89 per cent of class teachers in Reading Recovery schools, as opposed to 64 per cent in Phonological schools and 70 per cent in Control schools). They were also significantly more likely to work with books from a reading scheme (91 per cent as opposed to 70 per cent and 67 per cent), and to grade non-scheme books by level of difficulty (67 per cent as opposed to 41 per cent and 41 per cent). The class teachers in Reading Recovery schools were more likely to introduce children's reading books by discussing the vocabulary used in the books, by showing the children some of the words beforehand and by giving them an outline of the story. Finally, significantly more teachers in Reading Recovery schools reported using magnetic letters on a weekly basis for Year 2 children with reading difficulties. All of these significant differences between class teachers in Reading Recovery schools and the class teachers in other schools reflect central features of Reading Recovery practice.

9.2.2 Do these differences in classroom have an affect on children's reading progress?

It was possible to examine in a crude way[7] the relationship between these different classroom practices and the progress made by children in the study who were exposed to them. First, we selected the children who did not attend Reading Recovery schools. We then compared those children who were taught in classrooms where a particular practice was used with children taught in classrooms where it was not used to see if the practice bore any relationship to reading progress.[8]

---

[6] A Chi square analysis was used.

[7] Because of the small number of children in each class a multi-level model was difficult to apply, but because the factors were experienced at class level this would be the ideal form of analysis.

[8] A regression analysis was run, controlling for initial reading ability, with reading at first follow-up as the dependent variable to examine the effect of each activity on reading progress.

Table 9.1

Classroom practices more frequently reported in Reading Recovery schools, and their relationship to children's reading progress in the intervention year

Practice used	Classroom teachers % reporting the use of a practice		
	Reading Recovery schools (n of teachers = 43)	Phonological schools (n of teachers = 28)	Control schools (n of teachers = 20)
Use of running records as an assessment technique	89%	64%	70%
Use of reading schemes	91%	70%	67%
Grading of non-scheme books by level of difficulty	67%	41%	41%
Introducing the vocabulary of a book orally	78%	44%	55%
From the checklist of 49 reading activities	Percentage of teachers using this activity during the last week		
Label classroom objects	58%	30%	32%
Teacher asks questions during/after reading	69%	62%	39%
Teacher helps children to use context in reading	47%	16%	32%
Use of magnetic letters	25%	5%	7%
Learning whole words	53%	38%	41%
Constructing words	58%	40%	24%

The grading of non-scheme books by level of difficulty and the use of magnetic letters were significantly related to reading progress. Because of the rather crude nature of the information gathered on the classroom reading environment and the lack of significant relationships between other practices and progress, these results have to be viewed with caution. In the case of several other aspects of classroom practice there was not a sufficient variation between schools to test for a relationship between activity and progress. Some elements were complex, such as the way in which reading schemes, if adopted, were actually used. However, these results provide tentative evidence that some of the classroom practices which are more common in Reading Recovery schools are also related to reading progress in children.

9.3 The effect of the Phonological Intervention on the teaching of reading in the classroom

Teachers who administered the Phonological Intervention were instructed not to discuss their teaching techniques in the Phonological schools. It is therefore not surprising that 75 per cent of the classroom teachers in the schools who completed the questionnaire reported that their teaching methods had not been influenced by the intervention. There were no particular differences between the classroom practices in Phonological schools as compared with the other schools, other than those which can be seen in **Table 9.1**. None of these differences related to better progress in children's reading.

9.4 Conclusion

The study of classroom practice was not the central focus of the present study, as it has been for other researchers.[9] The interventions being evaluated were taught outside the classroom by specialist staff with specialist training. Nonetheless, it was of interest to investigate the extent to which the interventions influenced what happened in the classroom. In this context the class teachers in the 127 classrooms sampled[10] were asked to report their instructional practices rather than their beliefs about reading, as there is evidence to suggest that there may be little connection between the two,[11] and we were interested in what children actually experienced. The teachers' recollections are likely to be only a rough guide to classroom environment but, despite these limitations, the information collected allowed us to infer something about the nature of the teaching in the three types of schools: Reading Recovery, Phonological and Control.

As we had expected a large proportion of class teachers in the Reading Recovery schools reported that the presence of the intervention in their school had altered the way they taught reading in the classroom. This was in contrast to the situation in the Phonological schools where most teachers reported that the Phonological Intervention had no influence on their classroom practice. The teachers' impressions were confirmed by the finding that where significant differences did exist between Reading Recovery school classrooms and the classrooms of the other schools, they were in areas of practice which reflected central features of Reading Recovery.

---

[9] Eg Tizard et al, 1988, Blatchford & Ireson, 1994.

[10] Ie classrooms attended by the children participating in the study.

[11] Duffy and Anderson, 1981.

There are two reasons why this investigation is important. Firstly, the effectiveness of both interventions have in part been assessed by comparing Intervention children with Control children in the same schools, the within schools comparison. As demonstrated in Chapter 5 it was in the within schools comparisons that intervention effects were least apparent. In the case of the Phonological Intervention there were no significant within school intervention effects at either first or second follow-up. Reading Recovery also did not appear to have a significant effect on reading progress at second follow-up in the within school comparisons. The lack of within school effects, as opposed to the significant between school effects (where Intervention children were compared with Control children attending different schools) can be interpreted in at least two ways. Lack of significant effects may simply mean that the intervention is not effective. However, if some elements of the intervention have 'leaked' into the classroom and indirectly influenced Control children then the lack of a significant difference between Intervention and Control children within Reading Recovery can be seen as the result of programme 'leakage'. This is supported by the comparison between Intervention children and Control children attending different schools, which showed better progress in Reading Recovery children.

In the case of Reading Recovery we know that systematic efforts were made to disseminate various elements of Reading Recovery practice throughout the schools involved. We were able to detect evidence of this dissemination in Reading Recovery school classrooms and also some suggestion that exposure to these practices improved children's reading progress. Thus the 'leakage' interpretation has considerable support. In the case of the Phonological Intervention the evidence for this second interpretation was much less persuasive. The teacher/researchers who delivered the intervention were specifically told not to share details of their work with school staff. Most of the class teachers themselves reported that the presence of the intervention had made no difference to their teaching methods and we could observe few differences between Phonological school classrooms and the classrooms in the other schools on examining the class teachers' questionnaires.

Secondly, there are other reasons in favour of a better understanding of the impact of Reading Recovery on classroom practice and these concern cost effectiveness. The data presented in the present chapter offer some support for this potential benefit. However, there was no *significant* difference in reading progress between the Control children in Reading Recovery schools and those attending other schools.

There is, in fact, a third interesting avenue of investigation, not possible with the present data, which concerns the interaction effect between classroom and intervention. Reading Recovery was developed in New Zealand in a context where classrooms shared many common principles with Reading Recovery. However, as the programme has been exported to other countries this may be less true. Wasik and Slavin (1993), in their review of one-to-one tutoring programmes identify the potential importance of integrating between the tutoring programme and classroom instruction seen in 'Success for All'. In the case of the Phonological Intervention, which offers only one element of a full reading programme, the content of the classroom reading programme may have considerable bearing on the effectiveness of the intervention.

If Reading Recovery has a beneficial effect which extends beyond the target children to the school this will have a bearing on the cost effectiveness of the programme.

CHAPTER 10

THE EFFECTS OF READING RECOVERY ON AREAS OF CHILDREN'S BEHAVIOUR OTHER THAN READING

Evidence was reviewed in Chapter 1 that children with reading difficulties tend to fall behind in other areas and that their confidence in their own ability is undermined. This suggests that improving a child's reading will have wider reaching effects on their behaviour and skills. On the other hand we have seen that reading programmes tend to have a precise effect on the areas that they target and that, for example, a programme which focuses on developing reading accuracy may fail to have an effect on reading comprehension. If programmes have such a specific effect even within the same broad area of reading, it seems less likely that they can influence a child's behaviour in radically different domains. Bryant and Bradley certainly found that their Phonological Intervention had a specific effect on reading and spelling but did not improve children's maths attainments. In the present study we have seen that Reading Recovery had a strong effect on children's literacy skills. This offered us the opportunity to establish whether this successful intervention had effects specific to reading and writing or whether they extended to a wider range of children's behaviour and skill.

10.1 Behaviour problems

There is a well established tendency for behaviour problems and reading difficulties to co-exist.[1] What is unclear is the extent to which one causes the other. The current study offered an excellent opportunity to test whether helping children with their reading would have an impact on any behaviour problems that they might have. As we have demonstrated, Reading Recovery offered a very effective way of helping the children with their reading, especially in the short term. Information was also gathered from both their parents and their teachers on any behaviour problems they might have at the beginning of the study and at the first follow-up.[2] If some children respond to difficulty with their reading by developing some form of behaviour problem, improving their reading may also have an impact on their general behaviour. We could find no evidence that Reading Recovery had an effect on children's behaviour problems, either as reported by parents or teachers.

---

[1] See Chapter 6

[2] See Chapter 3.

10.1.1 Measurement of child behaviour problems

The Child Behaviour Questionnaire[3] consists of a number of behavioural descriptions for each of which the informant (parent or teacher) is asked to mark 'doesn't apply', 'applies somewhat' or 'certainly applies' to the child. Replies were given a weight of 0, 1 and 2 respectively and scores for individual items were added to obtain a total score. A measure of hyperactivity can be obtained by summing the score of three items: (i) 'very restless, often running about or jumping up and down, hardly ever still'; (ii) 'squirmy, fidgety child'; and (iii) 'cannot settle to anything for more than a few moments'.

There was a high response rate from teachers at both pre-test and first follow-up (91 per cent and 93 per cent respectively). The response from parents was less complete (54 per cent and 47 per cent respectively).

Ratings of the children's behaviour by their parents and by their teachers on the same occasion were found to correlate significantly but not highly (0.27 at pre-test; 0.40 at first follow-up), which is consistent with other research findings. It is quite possible that the children's behaviour is objectively different in the different settings. Ratings from the same informant at pre-test and first follow-up were both significantly and highly correlated (0.71 for the teacher rating and 0.72 for the parent rating). In other words a child's behaviour at six years was highly predictive of their behaviour nine months later within the same setting.

10.1.2 The effect of Reading Recovery on children's behaviour problems

As before, Reading Recovery children were compared with both Control children attending the same schools (the within school comparison) and with children attending different schools (the between schools comparison). All three groups of children had very similar scores on the CBQ at the beginning of the study and there was little change in the mean scores apparent at first follow-up (**Table 10.1**). The CBQ scores at follow-up in the two sets of comparisons were analysed, controlling for initial reading ability and behaviour problems. There was no evidence that Reading Recovery had any effect on behaviour.[4]

---

[3] Rutter, 1967; Rutter et al, 1970, 1975 and 1976.

[4] A regression analysis was used for both parent and teacher ratings separately for total score on the CBQ and for the hyperactive syndrome.

Table 10.1

Children's behaviour problems at the beginning of the study
and at first follow-up, by experimental condition

Experimental condition	Behaviour problems Mean scores and (standard deviations)			
	Pre-test		First follow-up	
	Teacher	Parent	Teacher	Parent
Reading Recovery children	7 (7)	9(6)	6 (6)	9(6)
Within school controls	6 (6)	8 (7)	6 (6)	10 (9)
Between school controls	6 (6)	9 (6)	7 (6)	8 (6)

10.2 School Absence

During preliminary discussions with schools it was suggested that the school attendance of children given Reading Recovery improved. Bearing in mind the fact that absence from school was found to disrupt children's reading progress this was a potentially useful side effect of the programme. We tested for this by comparing the number of days children on Reading Recovery were absent in the summer term 1993 with the rate of absence of the Control children (both within and between schools), taking account of initial reading ability and rate of absence in the summer term 1992.[5] There was no evidence of any intervention effect on absence.

10.3 Mathematics

It was of interest to test what effect, if any, Reading Recovery had on another area of the curriculum. Bryant and Bradley (1985) in their study of the effects of a Phonological Intervention very similar to the one used in the present research looked at intervention effects on maths as well as reading. Although they found that the intervention was a very good way of improving reading and spelling, it had no effect on children's maths skills. They argued that an intervention designed to improve reading and spelling should have a specific effect, and that a generalised effect would make the results more difficult to interpret. However, from a different perspective it has been argued that reading difficulties prevent progress in other areas of the curriculum, which frequently rely on an adequate level of reading. If this were the case any improvement in reading should lead to an improvement in these other curriculum areas.

---

[5] A regression analysis was used.

We compared Reading Recovery children's progress in maths with that of the within and between Control school children. Children's maths ability had been assessed at pre-test and second follow-up. Using a regression analysis and controlling for initial reading and maths ability, children's maths scores at second follow-up were compared. There was no evidence that Reading Recovery had any effect on children's progress in maths. It is still possible that other areas of the curriculum which involve more reading would be affected by an improvement in reading skills but this remains to be investigated.

10.4 Conclusion

There is no evidence that Reading Recovery is an effective intervention for improving either a child's behaviour problems, their school attendance or their performance in maths. The effect of the successful reading intervention seems to be specific to reading, at least at this stage. It would seem that children learn quite precisely what they are taught. However, because of the tendency for both behaviour problems and maths difficulties to co-exist with reading difficulties it was reasonable to investigate whether improving children's reading could also have an influence on these other aspects of their functioning. The fact that a successful reading intervention did not have such an effect suggests that reading failure is not a primary cause of either behaviour problems or difficulty with mathematics.

CHAPTER 11

SUMMARY AND CONCLUSION

In the foregoing chapters we have presented the results of an evaluation of two one-to-one interventions designed to help young children with reading difficulties: Reading Recovery and a specifically Phonological Intervention. The extensive literature reviewed indicates both that early problems with reading tend to remain, even intensify, as children grow and that their performance in other areas is increasingly affected. The research evidence on interventions designed to help such children indicates that the most effective ones are normally offered to children in the first years of schooling. It would seem that in the case of reading problems 'prevention' is better than 'cure'.

The interventions that we have evaluated have both been found to be effective in other studies, in the case of Reading Recovery in several other studies.[1] In the present study 180 children with initial reading difficulties were offered one or other of these interventions and compared with approximately 200 control children. Both the 91 children who received the Phonological Intervention and the 89 who went on the Reading Recovery programme made significantly better progress in various aspects of reading and writing than similar children who were not given any standardised intervention (the control group). This is in spite of the fact that the control children, who also had reading difficulties, did receive quite substantial amounts of specialised help with reading by their schools' special needs staff. Effects of both interventions on the children's reading progress were statistically significant one year after all intervention had been completed.

However, the two interventions were not equally effective. Reading Recovery was the more powerful one. First, Reading Recovery is aimed at a broader range of literacy skills than the Phonological Intervention. Consistent with this, we found Reading Recovery to be extremely effective across the whole range of reading and writing skills assessed whereas the Phonological Intervention initially had a specific effect on phonological awareness and writing. The effect of the Phonological Intervention broadened to take in word recognition and prose reading accuracy (but not prose comprehension) at second follow-up, one year after the completion of the programme. The more specific Phonological Intervention with its narrower focus was never designed to be a child's sole source of reading instruction.[2] Secondly, in areas of reading and writing where both interventions were effective Reading Recovery invariably produced greater gains overall than the Phonological Intervention. One probable reason for this lies in the fact that Reading Recovery helps children to integrate a wide range of skills involved in reading and writing, whereas the Phonological Intervention is more limited in its ability to enable children to cement these important links. In addition, children on Reading Recovery

---

[1] See Appendix 1.

[2] See Chapter 5.

received about three times as much one-to-one tuition as children taught the Phonological Intervention

There seems to be some truth in the old adage 'you get what you pay for' in intervention. This conclusion is supported by the review of other successful one-to-one programmes published by Wasik and Slavin (1993). These authors found several interventions, including Reading Recovery, to be effective, but none of them were substantially less intensive than Reading Recovery and therefore any cheaper. In the course of the present study we took a preliminary look at other UK reading initiatives funded by the Department for Education. The information available was in most cases not sufficient to make any useful comparisons with Reading Recovery or the Phonological Intervention. However, one initiative, the Leeds 'Sustained Reading Intervention' did present preliminary evidence suggesting that it might be an effective intervention. But this intervention was also an intensive one-to-one programme with considerable areas of overlap with Reading Recovery. From the information available the cost per child of the Leeds project was probably in excess of Reading Recovery.[3]

However, this does not tell the whole story. There are also reports in the literature of many interventions which fail to improve children's reading progress significantly.[4] In the present study there was no relationship between the amount of specialised help offered to the control children overall and the amount of progress they made in reading and writing. On the same theme of value for money, interventions of similar intensity do not always have equally powerful results.[5] Taking an example of an intervention of particular relevance to the present project, Hatcher and his colleagues (1994) compared children who received one-to-one tuition in a broad range of reading skills, including a specific and explicit phonics element, with children who received tuition in the phonics area alone. In this study both groups of children received the same *amount* of tuition. Those who received the broader programme made significantly greater progress in reading than those on the narrow phonics programme. On the other side of the coin Iversen and Tumner (1993) found that ensuring that there was a systematic coverage of phonics in each Reading Recovery session allowed children to graduate from the programme more rapidly than children offered the conventional programme. And in a similar vein Hatcher and his colleagues (1994) found that the effectiveness of their reading intervention, which was based on Reading Recovery, was enhanced by the inclusion of an additional systematic phonic element in each session. Subsequent to these investigations the phonic content of Reading Recovery sessions has in fact been strengthened over the last two years. What does seem to hold true is that strong and long lasting effects on the progress of children with reading difficulties are unlikely to be achieved without intensive and, therefore costly programmes. The reverse is not the case, that is that costly programmes inevitably produce good results.

---

[3] Relevant documents were obtained from the DfE.

[4] See Chapter 1 for a discussion.

[5] See Chapter 8.

In the USA, where substantial sums are spent on 'retention' and remedial programmes Philip Dyer (1992) has demonstrated that Reading Recovery has actually saved money for the school system by reducing the proportion of children who were required to repeat a year of their schooling. Here in the UK it is early days to see how Reading Recovery will affect other areas of spending in the special needs area. However, it is already clear from the present study that considerable amounts of specialised provision are made for young children with reading difficulties, in the absence of Reading Recovery. What is more, this provision, though substantially less expensive than Reading Recovery in the short term, not only produces much less impressive results but is also made available to the same children year after year. It seems likely that in the long run Reading Recovery will cost little or no more than normal school provision for these poor readers.[6] The question is whether Reading Recovery will be more effective in improving children's reading progress in the long term. The answer to this question is still uncertain. The results available from other studies of the long term effects of Reading Recovery suggest that children do gain a long term advantage, but that the effects of the programme weaken over time. In the present study we have only followed the children up for one year after intervention ended. However, our results tend to confirm this picture. It would be of great interest to follow the progress of the present sample of children and the special provisions they are offered for another year or two.

The Phonological Intervention, which costs little more than the standard specialist provision available to the control group, did produce greater effects on reading and spelling in one of the two comparisons with control children. Intriguingly, these effects were only statistically significant one year after the intervention had ended and not immediately after the intervention. It is difficult to anticipate what the long term effects might be. Again, it would be interesting to find out.

The Phonological Intervention was in general equally effective for all types of children, though slightly less powerful for those who started the study as complete non-readers (about half of the sample). It has been shown that Reading Recovery was a very powerful intervention for this group of non-readers, and also for children who were socially disadvantaged. It seemed likely that many of these children had only a limited previous experience of books. The daily exposure to several books during the Reading Recovery session may have redressed this balance. It has long been known that children from socially disadvantaged backgrounds are at risk of having difficulties with reading. These children and those that make the slowest starts in reading have been found in the USA to be particularly difficult to help.[7] An intervention which can produce long term effects on their reading progress is of great significance and this may be one reason that Reading Recovery is becoming increasingly widespread in the USA.

---

[6] Chapter 8 presents an analysis of cost effectiveness.

[7] Carter, 1984; Kennedy et al, 1986.

The fact that there is some evidence from the present study to suggest that Reading Recovery is particularly effective for the poorest readers also has implications for its effectiveness as a general, whole school reading programme. There has been a feeling in the UK that, beyond being a programme for children with reading difficulties, Reading Recovery might become a vehicle to import good reading practice into the classroom. Marie Clay has consistently argued that Reading Recovery is designed for children with reading difficulties and not for children managing adequately with classroom instruction. Whilst in the present study we have found that some of the general principles of Reading Recovery have taken root in the school as a whole, probably to some advantage, the specifics of the programme are most effective with the least able readers.

There has been considerable speculation concerning the components of Reading Recovery which make it so effective. Some have argued that any teaching programme which offers daily one-to-one tuition over a period of months would be equally valuable. But the research evidence both from the USA[8] and from the UK[9] where children have been given just such programmes does not support this hypothesis. And yet, critics argue, there is nothing unique about Reading Recovery. We find this very plausible, since each element of a Reading Recovery session may well be found in another context. What makes Reading Recovery so powerful is the structure which ensures a broad and systematic coverage of reading instruction taught with skill and pace. Not only has the content of the sessions been carefully developed but a similarly thoughtful approach has been taken to selection of children for the programme, teacher training and programme monitoring, thus ensuring that good practice is supported and maintained. There may indeed be nothing very remarkable about good practice but to be able to reproduce it year after year in lessons throughout the country would produce remarkable results. However, some essential elements of Reading Recovery are clear. A purely phonics approach does not produce such good results[10] but a strong phonic element *within* the broader programme of Reading Recovery is vital.[11]

The Phonological Intervention, though a less powerful method of improving the progress of young children than Reading Recovery, still had some significant effects on reading and writing one year after the intervention had been completed. It is a less expensive intervention than Reading Recovery and may be as effective for slightly better readers in the longer term. There is little doubt that some kind of explicit phonics instruction is an important ingredient in a programme. However, in the USA there is evidence that phonics tends to be taught through worksheets or exercises rather than in direct interaction with

---

[8] Pinnell et al, 1994.

[9] Hatcher et al, 1994.

[10] Both on the basis of Hatcher et al, 1994, and on the strength of our own findings on the Phonological Intervention.

[11] Hatcher et al, 1994; Iversen and Tunmer, 1993.

the teacher.[12] It is known that some children find it hard to concentrate or work well in these circumstances. For these children, or for children who have failed to make the necessary links between their phonological awareness and reading and writing, or indeed in schools where there is little explicit phonics instruction in the classroom, the Phonological Intervention may be particularly effective.

Finally, it is of interest that the children participating in the study, by and large, learnt what they were taught and not more. Although both interventions were successful in varying degrees in the area of reading and writing they had no measurable effect on either the children's maths progress or on their behavioural problems.

We finish as we began, by emphasising that the subject of this evaluation is of great importance. Children who have reading difficulties in our society suffer. As adults they are disadvantaged and may cost society dear. Both on grounds of compassion and common sense the prevention of reading difficulties in children must be a priority. In the foregoing evaluation we have demonstrated that it is possible to tackle this problem effectively. We hope that our findings will be put to good use.

---

[12] Adams, 1990.

APPENDIX 1

A REVIEW OF EVALUATION STUDIES OF THE READING RECOVERY PROGRAMME

J.D. DEMETRE

1. Aims

This report aims to review the evidence on the effectiveness of the Reading Recovery Programme (RRP). The RRP is an intervention programme devised by Clay (1985) for children who show difficulties in reading and writing at the end of their first year in primary school. The review draws on evidence from large-scale trials and controlled experimental evaluation studies. Evidence from case studies (eg Escamilla & Andrade, 1992; Lyons, 1991; Pinnell, 1989) and small scale pilot studies (eg Pluck, 1989) will not be reviewed, as their findings neither conflict with, nor add breadth to, the conclusions that can be drawn from the larger scale studies. An outline of the main features of each of the major studies is provided in the Appendix. The central focus of the review will be on outcomes in reading and writing performance, rather than on attitudinal changes in children (eg Cohen, McDonell & Osborn, 1989) or teachers (eg Geekie, 1992).

2. Assessment of reading and writing ability

The Diagnostic Survey and Book Level (Clay, 1985) are used both to identify and monitor children in need of remedial instruction, and as a research instrument for assessing outcome. There are wide differences in the composition and range of test instruments used in different investigations, but most use at least Book Level and several of the sub-tests comprising the Diagnostic Survey.

2.1 The Diagnostic Survey and Book Level

Book Level

A graded series of books is used to assess the highest level at which a child can read accurately (typically defined as 90 per cent accuracy on a running record). Levels range between 0-24 in the original New Zealand version, though both fewer and more levels have been used by different investigators.

The Diagnostic Survey comprises five sub-tests:

(1)   Letter Identification

   The number of upper-case and lower-case letters of the alphabet correctly identified. Scores range between 0-54.

(2) Concepts about Print

Assesses children's understanding of the conventions of written language, eg direction of reading print, units of print, such as letters, words. Scores range between 0-24.

(3) Word Test (Reading Vocabulary)

The number of frequently occurring words that a child can read out of context.

(4) Writing Vocabulary

The number of words that can spontaneously and accurately be written in 10 minutes.

(5) Dictation

Accuracy in writing a sentence from dictation. Scores range from 0-37.

Typically, 6-year-old children scoring in the bottom 20 per cent of their class on the Diagnostic Survey and Book Level are considered for induction into the RRP.

2.2 Reliability and validity

The comprehensive nature of the Diagnostic Survey in tandem with the Book Level makes it a useful instrument both for assessing children and for evaluating the outcome of interventions. There is some evidence concerning the important qualities of reliability and validity of Book Level and of some of the sub-tests comprising the Diagnostic Survey. Reliability refers to the consistency with which a test can be used to grade a group of individuals. For example, if a test is administered twice to a group of individuals, and their relative ranking on the test is very similar on the two occasions, then we have met an important criterion for reliability. Validity refers to the relevance of a test. For example, if children's relative rankings on a dictation test are similar to their relative rankings on a National Curriculum Assessment of reading (eg English 2), then we have met one criterion that the dictation test is a valid test of literacy skills.

Book Level (Clay, 1985) and Dictation (Pinnell et al, 1991) have been shown to meet the usual criteria of reliability and validity. The Word tests appear very similar to other tests of reading vocabulary (eg the Dolch Word Recognition Test, and the Burt Graded Word test), whose reliability and validity have been established.

However, it is possible that some of these tests may not be as reliable and valid in assessing post-intervention performance. It has yet to be established whether assessors' expectations about a child can significantly influence the child's score on each of these tests. In most of the evaluation studies reported, it is either clear that the assessors knew whether a given child had gone through a RRP, or no explicit details concerning post-intervention assessments are reported. In only one case is it explicitly stated that post-intervention assessments were carried out by independent assessors who were unaware of the children's intervention status (Pinnell et al, 1991).

2.3 The use of standardised tests

Some investigations have additionally administered standardised tests of reading and writing ability:

(1) Dolch Word Recognition Test: similar to the word tests in the Diagnostic Survey (used by Iversen & Tunmer, in press);

(2) Burt Graded Word test: similar to the word tests in the Diagnostic Survey (used by Clay, 1985; Wheeler, 1984; Wright, 1992);

(3) Woodcock Reading Mastery Test: comprises sub-tests of letter identification, word recognition and text comprehension. Scores on the sub-test are aggregated to yield a single measure of reading ability (used by Pinnell et al, 1991);

(4) Gates-MacGinitie Reading Test: a test administered to groups of children, comprising sub-tests of word recognition and text comprehension, again, yielding an aggregate score (used by Pinnell et al, 1991);

(5) Schonell (R1) Word Reading Test: a test of word recognition (used by Clay, 1985);

(6) Peters Word Spelling Test (used by Clay, 1985).

3. Effectiveness of the Reading Recovery programme (RRP)

Three criteria can be used to assess the effectiveness of the RRP: (1) in terms of the proportion of children who successfully complete the programme (when the child is adjudged to have attained a literacy level comparable to that of her/his 'average' peers - this criterion will be discussed more fully below); (2) whether such improvements are significantly greater than for comparable children who have not been in a RRP; (3) whether parity with peers in the average range of reading ability is sustained following termination of instruction. The evidence relating to each of these criteria is reviewed below in separate sub-sections.

APPENDICES

APPENDIX 1

3.1 Successful discontinuation and attainment of average literacy levels

Within 20 weeks of individualised Reading Recovery (RR) instruction, children are expected to read at average levels for their class or school, and be 'discontinued' from the programme, thereafter receiving only routine classroom instruction in reading. Children who do not meet this criterion are referred for special help, and are judged to have reading difficulties beyond the scope of the RRP.

Several studies report figures for the number of children who successfully meet discontinuation criteria in the RRP. However, in some reports, figures for the number of children who have not been successfully discontinued are aggregates of children who have not completed 20 weeks in RRP, children who have moved to a different location, as well as children who did not evince the requisite levels of improvement. **Table 1** contains a summary of data from field trials in which the numbers of children 'failing' in the RRP are specified. The figures appearing in the Table differ from those in the original reports, as I have taken as the number only the children who had completed RRP:

Table 1

Percentages of children failing in the RRP

Source	N in RRP	Fail
New Zealand (Clay, 1990)		
1984	2,164	5.92%
1985	3,331	7.15%
1986	4,896	7.35%
1987	6,217	5.03%
1988	6,884	5.67%
Ohio, USA (Groom et al, 1991)		
1991	5,708	11.00%
Surrey, UK (Wright, 1992)		
1990	35	5.7%
1991	44	2.27%

It would appear that the RRP meets its objectives with the overwhelming majority of children inducted into the programme. There is some evidence to suggest that the children failing to attain discontinuation criteria have among the lowest scores on the Diagnostic Survey (Wheeler, 1984; Wright, 1992).

While the proportion of children successfully meeting discontinuation criteria is impressively high, one must be clear about what these criteria signify. Typically, 'average' level refers to the mean initial scores of all children in a class (including children inducted into the RRP). Thus, there are two potential sources of overestimation of the RRP children's attainments at discontinuation: (1) the 'average' to which they are being compared is lower than the 'average' of children without reading difficulties; (2) because the 'average' is based on initial levels, the class average irrespective of intervention, is likely to be higher by the time the RRP children are discontinued. Three studies provide evidence that goes a long way in reducing concerns about the influence of these artifacts.

Groom et al (1991) in Ohio compared RRP children's scores with scores taken contemporaneously from a random sample of children attending schools in the state. Iversen and Tunmer (in press) in Rhode Island, USA used a matched-pairs design, where each RRP child was compared with a classmate who was adjudged to be in the middle range. Again, measures for the 'average' children were taken contemporaneously with discontinuation measures of RRP children. Wheeler (1984) in Victoria, Australia, compared RRP children's discontinuation scores with contemporaneous measures of all children sampled who were initially in the top 80 per cent on the Diagnostic Survey. The findings from these three studies are summarised in **Table 2**.

APPENDICES   APPENDIX 1

Table 2

Mean literacy scores for children in RRP and 'average' readers

Test	Survey	RRP N	Initial	Terminal	'Average' N	Terminal
Text Level	Groom et al (Max = 30)	3,860	0.81	19.31	66	17.76
	Wheeler (Max = 6)	94	1.47	5.84	410	5.49
Letter Ident. (Max = 54)	Iversen & Tunmer	32	42.38	52.78	32	52.81
	Wheeler	94	36.69	51.72	410	52.14
Concepts About Print (Max = 24)	Iversen & Tunmer	32	11.22	19.5	32	17.19
	Wheeler	94	11.58	19.36	410	19.50
Dictation (Max = 37)	Groom et al	3,860	8.87	35.39	66	33.73
	Iversen & Tunmer	32	11.25	34.00	32	32.72
	Wheeler	94	14.05	34.05	410	33.62
Writing Vocabulary	Groom et al	3,860	5.38	54.15	66	45.67
	Iversen & Tunmer	32	4.03	38.28	32	33.22
	Wheeler	94	6.85	43.09	410	44.84
Reading Vocabulary	Iversen & Tunmer (Diagnostic Survey, Max = 15)	32	0.91	12.16	32	12.13
	Iversen & Tunmer (Dolch Test, Max = 179)	32	4.19	93.81	32	99.59
	Wheeler (Burt Test, Max = 35)	94	3.7	24.02	410	31.41

In general, the mean scores of children successfully discontinued from the RRP appear to be comparable to those of variously defined 'average' readers. Furthermore, data presented by Groom et al indicate that over 88 per cent of RRP children score within or above the average band (mean of 'average' sample ± half a standard deviation) for each of the three sub-tests they administered. However, the authors do not report the percentage of 'average' children who score within or above this band. It is possible (albeit unlikely) that a significantly greater percentage of 'average' readers attain this criterion.

While there is a good degree of concordance in the findings of the three studies, there is also an interesting element of divergence apparent in the data. The achievements of RRP children tend to be somewhat less impressive relative to 'average' children in Wheeler's study. This is to be expected, as Wheeler took as 'average' the top 80 per cent of readers (one would expect 30 per cent to be below the population mean, and 50 per cent to be above the mean), Groom et al took a random sample (where one would expect an equal proportion to fall above and below the population mean), and Iversen and Tunmer sampled children presumed to be in the mid-range. Only in Wheeler's case, therefore, would one expect to find a relative surfeit of above-average scores relative to below-average scores. Thus, Wheeler's 'average' group makes for a particularly stringent criterion against which to gauge the success of the RRP.

3.2 Comparisons with control groups

The evidence summarised above may suggest that the RRP is a highly effective intervention procedure, elevating poor readers to average levels. However, it is possible that such improvement occurs spontaneously with the passage of time, and is not the direct result of the RRP. Comparison of RRP children's performance at discontinuation with that of comparably poor readers not receiving the RRP is an essential element of evaluation.

Very few studies have employed random allocation of children to treatments. For seemingly ethical considerations, some studies have selected 'control' children whose reading ability is greater than that of children assigned to the RRP. In such cases, the 'control' group comprises a heterogeneous mixture of higher-ability and lower-ability readers (eg Clay, 1985), or lower-ability readers who fall above the 20 per cent threshold for RRP (Glynn et al, 1989), or a very small sample showing a markedly mixed profile on the Diagnostic Survey (Wright, 1992). In these cases, it is not clear whether one should view the 'control' group as a control group (whose performance the RRP group should significantly surpass) or as a criterion group (whose performance the RRP group should match). This ambiguity has led to the utilisation of gain scores in comparing the RRP and 'control' groups. Typically, children in RRP gain bigger increases in the Diagnostic Survey sub-tests than 'controls', but absolute terminal scores are not consistently higher for the RRP.

The use of gain scores is likely to lead to an over-estimation of the relative gains of children whose initial scores are low (Iversen & Tunmer, in press). A number of the sub-tests comprising the Diagnostic Survey do not have interval scales: thus, gaining five book levels when proceeding from Book Level 1 to Book Level 6 ordinarily takes less time than proceeding from Book Level 19 to Book Level 24. I have undertaken an analysis of Glynn et al's raw data, and obtained a number of significant negative correlations between initial score and gain score, within both the RRP group and the 'control' group. In other words, children with relatively low initial scores tend to have relatively high gain scores, irrespective of whether they receive RRP or not. It then follows that as the RRP group on average has lower initial scores than the 'control' group, that on average they should also have higher gain scores than the 'control' group.

Two studies have used appropriate control groups. Studies in Ohio (eg Pinnell et al, 1991) and Rhode Island (Iversen & Tunmer, in press) show that children in RRP score significantly higher on various literacy measures at discontinuation than control children receiving 'usual' remedial instruction. Pinnell et al report the effect sizes and statistical significance of comparisons, but not the means. They found that the RRP group had significantly higher terminal scores than the control group on all four measures used: the Dictation test; a measure of text level; the Woodcock Reading Mastery Test; and the Gates-MacGinitie Reading Test.

Table 3 summarises the Iversen & Tunmer data, which are based on the Diagnostic Survey. The RRP group's scores were significantly greater than those of the control group in every sub-test administered in the terminal assessment. As to be expected, even the control children show improvements, but not as substantial as those of RRP children.

Table 3

Mean literacy scores for children in RRP and controls

(After Iversen & Tunmer)

	RRP		Control	
	Initial	Terminal	Initial	Terminal
Book Level (Max = 26)	0.53	16.43	0.56	3.00
Letter Identification (Max = 54)	42.38	52.78	43.13	48.86
Concepts About Print (Max = 24)	11.22	19.5	9.84	13.14
Dictation (Max = 37)	11.25	34.00	11.88	21.36
Writing Vocabulary	4.03	38.28	5.41	13.71
Reading Vocabulary (Diagnostic Survey, Max = 15) (Dolch Test, Max = 179)	0.91 4.19	12.16 93.84	1.41 5.25	4.71 17.00

The evidence from both studies is consistent in showing superiority of RRP children over controls. However, the particularly strong relative effect of group found for Book Level in the Iversen & Tunmer study (a difference of about 13 levels) is much greater than that reported in Pinnell et al (a difference of about six levels) for a similar measure.

3.3 Long-term maintenance of improvements

Follow-up studies generally employ fewer assessment tests, and usually rely on some measure of text reading level, analogous to the Book Level sub-test of the Diagnostic Survey. Follow-up studies of children successfully discontinued show these children to continue to make progress in the years following discontinuation (Clay, 1985; Reading Recovery Program, Ohio, 1991; Rowe, 1991). Moreover, the Ohio and Rowe reports show that RRP children's reading scores fall largely within the average band even two and five years (respectively) after discontinuation. Clay (1985) found that at three years post-discontinuation, the RRP group's mean on the Schonell Reading Test, the Burt Word Test, and the Peters Word Spelling test was age-appropriate.

There appear to be some vacillations between years: in the Ohio study, the mean level attained on graded texts by RRP children at three years post-discontinuation was at the bottom boundary of average readers; in Rowe's study in Australia, there appears to be a catch-up phenomenon, with the RRP mean increasingly resembling the mean of average readers, being almost identical in the four- and five-year post-discontinuation assessments. However, these apparent vacillations may very well signify no more than the random variability to be expected from repeated sampling.

Studies comparing the progress of RRP children with control children have produced an apparently inconsistent picture. Pinnell et al (1991) in a short-term follow-up (seven months post-discontinuation) found the statistical significance of differences between the two groups to be somewhat attenuated for text reading level, and markedly attenuated for their only other measure, performance on the Dictation test. Only one study has used an appropriate control group in a long-term follow-up assessment (Reading Recovery Program, Ohio, 1991). In this study, the absolute differences between the two groups on Book Level tended to *increase* with time. Moreover, improvements among the control children were substantial (see **Table 4** for a summary).

Table 4

Mean text level as a function of years from discontinuation

Years	RRP	Control
0	9	6
1	14	8
2	25	15
3	29	21

N.B. These are approximate figures taken from a graph.

The apparent inconsistency between the two studies can be resolved by inspection of **Table 4**. It appears that the mean differences between groups can be stable, or even increase with time, but this difference may account for less of the total variance than the differences between years. Put simply, children in RRP continue to show superiority over control children, but the latter also improve substantially. From the results in **Table 4**, it would appear that RRP children maintain on average a year's advantage over control children.

4. Adaptations and other forms of remediation

It was noted in the previous sections that children successfully discontinued from RRP outperform other poor readers receiving standard remedial services. How does the RRP compare with other specialised programmes? To date, studies have not directly contrasted the RRP with another programme.

Recently, Iversen & Tunmer (in press) predicted that a RRP that incorporated training in phonological processing (à la Bryant & Bradley, 1985) would be more effective than a standard RRP. Contrary to their prediction, the findings of Iversen & Tunmer's study showed that the two programmes produced very similar effects, with both programmes producing major improvements in Diagnostic Survey scores and scores on phonological processing measures. This parity was maintained at the end-of-year follow-up. However, discontinuation criteria were achieved faster in the RRP that incorporated phonological training (mean discontinuation after 41.75 lessons, compared with a mean of 57.31 lessons for the 'standard RRP').

An analogous study by Hatcher et al (1992) has shown that an experimental reading programme sharing some characteristics of the RRP produces more pronounced effects on standardised literacy measures when combined with training in phonological processing. However, while the findings from this study suggest that phonological training is an important component of effective literacy programmes, they have little bearing on the RRP proper. Standard RRPs *do* provide guidance in phonological aspects of reading, and it is for this reason that Iversen & Tunmer found significant changes in phonological processing measures following a 'standard' version of the RRP.

One particularly incisive study sought to test some of the different components of the RRP, and assess what aspects of the programme are effective. Pinnell et al (1991) contrasted children in a standard RRP programme, with three other treatment groups, as well as appropriate controls: (1) in a programme based on the RRP, but requiring only two weeks' training of teachers; (2) in a programme using one-to-one instruction, where teachers had no exposure to the RRP principles; (3) in an RRP programme in which children were instructed in groups. The only two groups to show significantly higher terminal scores than controls were the standard RRP group and the group instructed by teachers who had attended a short course on RRP. The standard RRP group showed superiority in all measures relative to controls and all other treatment groups. Moreover, only the RRP group showed superiority relative to controls in the seven-month follow-up assessment.

Clearly, the number of studies reviewed in this section is very small, and any conclusions drawn would perforce be premature. However, if these experiments are repeated and extended (eg how do children fare if trained in RRP by teachers who have received a short form of training in combination with training in phonological instruction), one could begin to think more systematically about the opportunity costs incurred by any given implementation.

5. Conclusion

The number of evaluation studies of the Reading Recovery Programme is small, but the findings, using the three criteria outlined at the beginning of the review, support the notion that the programme can dramatically improve the literacy skills of most poor readers, and enable them to progress along with their peers. While the evidence to date for the effectiveness of the Reading Recovery Programme is impressive, there are some shortcomings in the evaluation literature that need to be addressed. Some of these deficiencies have been discussed in the preceding sections of this report, but two particularly pressing issues need to be discussed:

1. From the studies reviewed, it would appear that over 5 per cent of children who enter a RRP are not significantly helped. In Groom et al's study, a further 5 per cent to 12 per cent (depending on the measure used) show significant improvements, but fall below the average band (ie below more than half a standard deviation from the average). While none of the available evidence speaks to this, it is also possible that with the passage of time from discontinuation, a further percentage subsequently fall below the average band. Given this pattern of outcomes, it would seem that some children are not as susceptible to the RRP as others.

   It was also noted in a previous section that poor readers who do not enter the RRP also show large gains in reading with age. Thus, perhaps the RRP can best be characterised as an intervention programme that accelerates the literacy skills of poor readers who would otherwise show some progress with existing remedial services. The corollary of this is that the RRP may be ineffective with particular kinds of children. It was previously noted that the available evidence suggests that the children who are not successfully discontinued from RR have particularly low initial scores on the Diagnostic Survey. Clearly, there is a need for investigators to undertake a more detailed study of these children, as well as of other children who show below-average improvements. More detailed characterisations of these children and their circumstances may provide clues for the design of supplementary or alternative intervention programmes.

2. The reports on long-term maintenance contain very few methodological details. Typically, there is no information on who administered the assessments, or on the attrition rates of samples. The information on the content of the text reading level assessments also tends to be scant. These reports lack in rigour of exposition, and one is left having to take the summarised data at face value.

These criticisms notwithstanding, the evidence suggests that the Reading Recovery Programme is a very promising intervention programme for 6 year old children who have difficulties mastering literacy skills. The remedial programmes provided for various children are likely to benefit from research that undertakes a more thorough analysis of the characteristics of children on whom the Reading Recovery Programme has a marginal impact. The incorporation of more explicit training in phonological processing skills into the Reading Recovery Programme may also yield dividends though, to date, only one study has addressed this issue directly.

6. References

Bryant, PE & Bradley, L *Children's Reading Problems*, Blackwell, Oxford (1985).

Clay, MM *The Early Detection of Reading Difficulties*, 3rd edition; Heinemann, Portsmouth (1985).

Clay, MM 'The Reading Recovery Programme, 1984-88: Coverage, outcomes and education board district figures' *New Zealand Journal of Educational Studies, 25*, 61-70 (1990).

Cohen, SG, McDonell, G & Osborn, B 'Self-perceptions of "at-risk" and high achieving readers: Beyond Reading Recovery achievement data.' in *Cognitive and Social Perspectives for Literacy Research and Instruction, National Reading Council Yearbook*, Washington DC (1989).

Escamilla, K & Andrade, A 'Descubriendo la Lectura: An application of Reading Recovery in Spanish' *Education and Urban Society*, 24, 212-226 (1992).

Geekie, P 'Reading Recovery: It's not what you do, it's the way you do it.' in N. Jones & E.B. Jones (Eds), *Learning to Behave: Curriculum and Whole School Management Approaches to Discipline*, Kogan Page, London (1992).

Glynn, T, Crooks, T, Bethune, N, Ballard K and Smith, J *Reading Recovery in Context*: Final report to the New Zealand Ministry of Education, Wellington, NZ (1989).

Groom, J, Lyons, C, Pinnell, GS, DeFord, D, Sullivan, M, Cai, M and Nilges, W *Ohio's Reading Recovery Program, Volume XIV*, State of Ohio, Columbus, Oh (1991).

Hatcher, P, Hulme, C and Ellis, A 'Overcoming early reading failure by integrating the teaching of reading and phonological skills: the phonological linkage hypothesis', paper submitted for publication (1992).

Iversen, S and Tunmer, WE (in press) 'Phonological Processing Skills and the Reading Recovery Programme', *Journal of Educational Psychology*.

Lyons, CA 'Reading Recovery: A viable prevention of learning disability', *Reading Horizons, 31*, 384-407 (1991).

Pinnell, GS 'Reading Recovery: helping at-risk children learn to read', *Elementary School Journal, 90*, 160-183 (1989).

Pinnell, G, Lyons, C, DeFord, D, Bryk, A and Seltzer, M *Studying the Effectiveness of Early Intervention Approaches for First Grade Children Having Difficulty in Reading*, Martha L. King Language and Literacy Center Educational Report No. 16., Ohio State University, Columbus, OH (1991).

Pluck, M-L 'Reading Recovery in a British infant school', *Educational Psychology, 9*, 347-358 (1989).

Reading Recovery Program, Ohio State University (1991). *The Reading Recovery Program: Executive Summary, 1984-91*, Ohio State University, Columbus, OH.

Rowe, KJ 'Students, parents, teachers and schools make a difference: A summary report of major findings from the "100 Schools Project" literacy programmes study', State Board of Education and School Programmes Division, Ministry of Education and Training, Victoria, Australia (1991).

Wheeler, HG *Reading Recovery: Central Victorian Field Trials*, Faculty of Education, Bendigo College of Advanced Education, Victoria, Australia (1984).

Wright, A 'Evaluation of the first British Reading Recovery Programme', *British Educational Research Journal, 18*, 351-368 (1992).

7. Appendix: A Summary of Reported Studies

CLAY (1985):

A study of 122 children in RRP in Auckland, New Zealand. Used all six sub-tests of the Diagnostic Survey at post-discontinuation, and contrasted gain scores with a 'control' group of somewhat better readers. Included long-term assessments: at one year post-discontinuation (using Book Level and Word Tests); and at three years post-discontinuation (using the Schonell Reading Test, the Burt Word Test and Peters Word Spelling Test).

CLAY (1990):

Presented annual returns from the New Zealand Department of Education over a five-year period. A total of 35,742 children had entered the RRP during this period. Reported on numbers of children successfully discontinued, unsuccessfully discontinued, still in the programme, and relocated.

APPENDICES

GLYNN ET AL (1989):

A study of 42 RRP children, in central Victoria, Australia. Compared RRP group's gain scores on Book Level with gains of a 'control' group of somewhat better readers.

GROOM ET AL (1991):

Presented an analysis of the attainments of 5,708 children in RRP in the state of Ohio, USA. Compared RRP children with a control group drawn at random from Ohio schools where RRP was not in operation. Discontinuation assessments comprised Writing Vocabulary, Dictation Test, and assessment of text reading level.

IVERSEN & TUNMER (IN PRESS):

Contrasted the progress of 32 children in a standard RRP programme with that of 32 children in a modified RRP programme which included training in phonological processing, and 32 controls. Children were sampled from schools in the state of Rhode Island, USA. Children in the three groups were matched in triplets in terms of initial performance on the Diagnostic Survey. In addition, criterion groups of 'average' readers, drawn from treatment subjects' school class, were assessed. Discontinuation and end-of-year follow-up assessments comprised the Diagnostic Survey, the Dolch Word Recognition Test, and three tests of phonological processing: the Yopp-Singer phoneme segmentation test; a phoneme deletion test; and phonological recoding (pseudoword decoding) test.

PINNELL ET AL (1991):

A study of 403 poor readers in Ohio. Children in a standard RRP programme (an unspecified number) were contrasted with four other groups: a programme based on the RRP, but requiring only two weeks' training of teachers; a programme using one-to-one instruction, where teachers had no exposure to the RRP principles; an RRP programme in which children were instructed in groups; and a control group. The discontinuation assessments comprised the Dictation Test, a measure of text reading level, the Woodcock Reading Mastery Test, and the Gates MacGinitie Reading Test. A seven-month post-discontinuation assessment was undertaken, comprising the Dictation Test and a measure of text reading level.

READING RECOVERY PROGRAM, OHIO STATE (1991):

Presented results on 136 children who had been successfully discontinued from RRP in Columbus, Ohio. Data presented on text reading level for three successive post-discontinuation years and compared with the text reading levels of a control group of poor readers, and the average band of a criterion group of children randomly sampled from the state.

ROWE (1991):

Reported data on reading bands of several cohorts of children who had gone through the RRP in Victoria. For one cohort, levels of progress up to five years post-discontinuation were reported, along with the progress of 'average' children.

WHEELER (1984):

A study of 134 RRP children in Victoria, Australia. Compared RRP children's gain scores on the Diagnostic Survey sub-tests and the Burt Word Test with gain scores of another group of children (the top 80 per cent of readers sampled).

WRIGHT (1992):

A study of two cohorts of children going through the RRP in Surrey (n=38 and 44, respectively). Children's discontinuation scores on all sub-tests of the Diagnostic Survey and Burt Word Test compared with pre-test scores, and gain scores compared with those of a very small 'control' group (n=8) with a mixed profile of pre-test performance. Unlike other studies, children inducted into RRP scored in the bottom 30 per cent (as opposed to the more usual 20 per cent) of the Diagnostic Survey. National Curriculum Assessments were also administered at the end of the school year. An estimate of the average cost of RRP per child is provided: £600-£800.

APPENDIX 2

TRAINING IN PHONOLOGICAL AWARENESS

The aim of the training is to encourage the child to listen to and categorise words that have a common sound. Initially pictures are used. Always get the child to name the pictures and correct any mistakes.

Check that the child understands terms such as 'beginning', 'end', 'start', 'first', 'sound'. Introduce such words along with the pictures and ask the child for information about the pictures in a variety of ways so that the child becomes familiar with the terminology.

Begin each session by revising previous sounds. Use the oddity game to revise sounds if the child is able to perform this. Encourage the child to produce additional words in the appropriate sound sets.

Encourage the child to explain what he or she is doing.

Depending on the child's response, aim at introducing one or two sounds per session, some initial and some final.

1. Initial Sounds (Levels 1, 2, 3)

Order of sound presentation 'c', 'm' in level 1, 'b', 't' in level 2 and 'h', 'n' in level 3.

Present the child with pictures from the set of pictures of things which share a given sound (about three pictures). Let the child identify the common sound and find further examples. When the initial sound is easily recognised use different cards from the same set to ensure that it is the sound, not the particular picture that is being identified.

- a) Can you tell me something about these pictures? What is the same about these pictures? What sound to do these pictures begin with?

- b) Find me pictures of things that start the same as this one.

- c) Find me pictures of things that start with e.g. 'c'.

Choose a group of pictures with a common sound and one with a different sound.

- d) Which picture doesn't start with the same sound as the others?

- e) Which pictures go together? Why?

- f) If a child has some letter knowledge then letters can be introduced. Always provide help and corrective feedback. Encourage the child to discover and discuss common letter patterns.

1) What letters could we use to spell this word? What does it start with (Choose a picture from the set of pictures with the common sound).
2) Can you find that letter amongst these letters? (Show the child no more than nine possible letters. Try and avoid confusable letters initially.)
3) Let's make another word. (Choose another picture from the same sound set. Repeat 1) and 2) for this word). Does that have any letters the same as eg 'cup'? What letters are the same? They both have the same letter at the start ! So we don't need to change the first letter. What other words will start with this letter?

Give lots of praise and provide a correct model for the child if necessary. Repeat with other words from the same set. Encourage the child to place the letters themselves and to notice any letters that remain the same. Encourage the child to explain where words have sounds and letters in common.

g) Oddity game. Present the child with three cards, two beginning with the same sound and one beginning with a different sound (a sound already taught if possible). Ask the child to say which card does not belong with the others and why. Use different picture cards for the cards which share a common sound. Put the 'odd' card in a different position in front of the child each time. If the child is able, encourage him or her to create his or her own oddity set using the cards in front of him or her.

Repeat stages a) to g) without pictures. Ask child to think of other things beginning with that sound.

2. Rhyme (Levels 4 and 5)

Order of sound presentation 'at' and 'en' in level 4, 'ill' and 'and' in level 5. Introduce the concept of rhyme using Nursery Rhymes. Ask the child if they know any nursery rhymes and let them supply the last word of the line eg 'Jack and Jill went up the ...'.

Repeat stages a) to e) for rhyming words. Check that the child understands that the words have a common sound at the end.

h) If a child has some letter knowledge then letters can be introduced. Always provide help and corrective feedback. Encourage the child to discover and discuss common letter patterns.

1) What letters could we use to spell this word? What does it start with? Can you hear any other letters? (Choose a picture from the set of pictures with the end common sound).
2) Can you find the letter among these letters? (Show the child no more than nine possible letters. Try and avoid confusable letters initially.)

3) Let's make another word. (Choose another picture from the set of pictures with the same end sound. Repeat 1) and 2) for this word). Does that have any letters the same as eg 'cat'? What letters are the same? They both have the same letter at the end and the middle! So we don't need to change those letters. We just have to change the first letter. What other words can we make with these letters at the end?

Give lots of praise and provide a correct model for the child if necessary. Repeat with other words from the same set. Encourage the child to place the letters him or herself and to notice any letters that remain the same. Encourage the child to explain where words have sounds and letters in common.

i) Rhyme oddity games. The oddity game can be played in a variety of ways when dealing with end sounds and can become increasingly more sophisticated.

1st. Let the odd word out be completely different from the two words with a common end sound eg 'hen', 'pen', 'ball'
2nd. Let the odd word have a common vowel eg 'hen', 'pen', 'leg'.

3. End Sound (Levels 6 and 7)

These levels will only be reached after children have shown themselves to be competent at rhyme (showing clear awareness of the onset-rime distinction). If you are in doubt do not move on to end sounds without comprehensive revision of the previous levels.

Order of sound presentation 'n' and 't' in Level 6, 'n', 't' and 'g' in Level 7. Introduce the concept of a common final sound via a version of the oddity game.

j) End sound oddity game.

1st. Let the two common words rhyme and the odd word have a different end sound eg 'mat', 'rat', 'bag'.
2nd. Let the two common words share just the same final sound eg 'pin', 'gun', 'bell'.

Repeat stages a) to e) for end sounds.

k) If a child has some letter knowledge then letters can be introduced. Always provide help and corrective feedback. Encourage the child to discover and discuss common letter patterns.

1) What letters could we use to spell this word? What does it start with? Can you hear any other letters? (Choose a picture from the set of pictures with the common sound).

2) Can you find that letter amongst these letters. (Show the child no more than nine possible letters. Try and avoid confusable letters initially).

3) Let's make another word (Choose another picture from the same sound set. Repeat 1) and 2) for this word). Does that have any letters the same as e.g. 'gun'? What letters are the same? They both have the same letter at the end! So we don't need to change the last letter. What other words will end with this letter?

Give lots of praise and provide a correct model for the child if necessary. Repeat with other words from the same set. Encourage the child to place the letters him or herself and to notice any letters that remain the same. Encourage the child to explain where words have sounds and letters in common.

4. Revise and Expand

Following the three stages above introduce new sets using the pictures and additional word sets in order to build up a knowledge of sound categorisation. Only move on to vowel categorisation if the child has no difficulty with the above.

5. Vowel sound

Introduce the concept of a common vowel sound via a version of the oddity game.

1) Vowel sound oddity game.

1st. Let the two common words rhyme and the odd word have a different vowel but the same end sound eg 'man', 'hen', 'pen'. Encourage the child to discuss what is the same about the words. They are the same at the end so where does the difference lie?

2nd. Let the two common words share just the same vowel sound eg 'ball', 'peg', 'men'.

Repeat stages a) to e) for vowel sounds. Repeat word building with letters, stage k), for words with common vowel sounds.

APPENDIX 3

TABLES

Table A3.1

Initial measures as predictors (correlates) of performance at 1st follow-up*

Initial measures	Follow up measures			
	Word Reading	Prose Reading	Book Level	Diagnostic Survey
Word Reading	.75	.73	.68	.56
Prose Reading	.84	.69	.71	.52
Book Level	.61	.61	.57	.47
Diagnostic Survey	.73	.72	.70	.75

Table A3.2

Initial measures as predictors (correlates) of performance at 2nd follow-up*

Initial measures	Follow up measures					
	Word Reading	Prose Reading (Accuracy)	Prose Reading (Comp)	Spelling	Phonological skills (Kirtley)	Non-word reading
Word Reading	0.62	0.63	0.66	0.59	0.37	0.46
Prose Reading	0.55	0.54	0.60	0.54	0.33	0.38
Book Level	0.47	0.46	0.48	0.48	0.31	0.51
Diagnostic Survey	0.69	0.66	0.65	0.67	0.45	0.51
Phon. Awareness (Kirtley)	0.23	0.23	0.27	0.27	0.35	0.21

* Correlations were performed on 274 children's scores. The Reading Recovery children were excluded as we knew that the intervention effect would mask the relationship between reading at different time points.

APPENDIX 4

THE RESULTS OF A MULTILEVEL MODELLING ANALYSIS

1. Reading Recovery: within school analyses, first follow-up

1.1 Progress: Book Level

These results are based on those 17 schools with control children and on those children with data on free school meals – there are 35 control and 62 RR children (n = 97). The RR group is 0.77 sd units behind at pre-test and 1.8 levels (or 0.29 sd units) ahead at post-test.

About 22 per cent of the total variation is variation between schools but between school variation is very small after controlling for the pre-test (ie the Diagnostic Survey).

After controlling for the pre-test, the group effect is 4.6 levels or 0.73 sd units ($\chi^2 = 24.5, 1, p < 0.001$).

The inclusion of the free school meals variable and its interaction with group improves the fit of the model ($\chi^2 = 8.41, 2, p < 0.02$) and a further improvement is then obtained by including the square of the pre-test ($\chi^2 = 4.7, 1, p < 0.04$). The group effect is 7.2 levels or 1.2 sd units when receiving free meals, 2.1 levels or 0.34 sd units when not receiving meals.

The effect of the language variable is small and there is no evidence of any interaction between group and pre-test.

1.2 Progress: Word Reading

The response variable here is the square root of the BAS at post-test. There are 34 control children and 63 RR children (n = 97). The RR group is 0.78 sd units behind at pre-test and 0.09 sd units ahead at post-test.

About 19 per cent of the total variation is variation between schools but between school variation is essentially zero after controlling for the pre-test.

After controlling for the pre-test (both linear and quadratic terms), the group effect is 0.60 sd units ($\chi^2 = 11.3, 1, p < 0.001$).

The inclusion of the free school meals variable and its interaction with group improves the fit of the model ($\chi^2 = 9.8, 2, p < 0.01$). The group effect is 1.0 sd units when receiving free meals, 0.24 sd units when not receiving meals.

The effect of the language variable is small. There is no firm evidence for an interaction between group and pre-test ($\chi^2 = 4.46, 2, p > 0.10$).

1.3 Progress: Prose Reading

The response variable here is the square root of the Neale at post-test. There are 34 control children and 58 RR children in 16 schools (n = 92). The RR group is 0.76 sd units behind at pre-test and 0.09 sd units **behind** at post-test.

About 17 per cent of the total variation is variation between schools but between school variation is essentially zero after controlling for the pre-test.

After controlling for the pre-test, the group effect is 0.38 sd units ($\chi^2 = 3.8, 1, p < 0.06$). The inclusion of the free school meals variable and its interaction with group improves the fit of the model ($\chi^2 = 7.3, 2, p < 0.03$). The group effect is 0.87 sd units when receiving free meals, **-0.05** sd units when not receiving meals.

There is no evidence for an interaction between group and pre-test.

1.4 Progress: Diagnostic Test

The response variable here is the Diagnostic Survey at post-test. There are 34 control children and 63 RR children in 17 schools (n = 97). The RR group is 0.86 sd units behind at pre-test and 0.10 sd units **ahead** at post-test.

About 22 per cent of the total variation is variation between schools but between school variation is very small after controlling for the pre-test (ie the Diagnostic Survey).

After controlling for the pre-test, the group effect is 0.64 sd units ($\chi^2 = 10.6, 1, p < 0.01$). The inclusion of the free school meals variable and its interaction with group improves the fit of the model less than for the other variables ($\chi^2 = 4.3, 2, p < 0.12$). The group effect is 1.0 sd units when receiving free meals, 0.34 sd units when not receiving meals.

There is no evidence of any interaction between group and pre-test.

1.5 Discussion

The following table summarises the results:

Variable	Overall	Free meals	No free meals
Book Level	0.73	1.2	0.34
Word Reading	0.60	1.0	0.24
Prose Reading	0.38	0.87	-0.05
Diagnostic	0.64	1.0	0.34

The interaction with free meals is consistent, if not always statistically significant. Although some schools have no children in the sample receiving free meals and in others all sample children are receiving free meals, similar results are obtained if these schools are omitted.

Some potentially interesting questions cannot be answered with these data: is the intervention effect consistent across schools (ie are all RR tutors equally effective?); is the association between pre-test and post-test the same for all schools? Also, the data set is rather small for picking up interactions between the pre-test and group, although we find no evidence for them.

2. Reading Recovery: between school analyses, first follow-up

All results are based on those schools (n = 57) with at least two pupils and on those pupils with data on the diagnostic test and information on free school dinners (n = 226/227). The RR pupils are those in the RR schools (n = 78); the control pupils are the control pupils in the 'phonological' schools plus those in the control schools (n = 148).

43 per cent of the control group received free school dinners; 40 per cent of the RR group.
16 per cent were ESL; 19 per cent of the RR group.
63 per cent boys; 59 per cent.

Because 'group' is defined at the school level here (level 2), rather than at the pupil level (level 1) as in the within school analyses, we first have to establish that there is between school variation to be explained **after** controlling for the pre-test(s) and any other possible explanatory variables, **and then** to see whether 'group' explains any of the remaining between school variation.

To replicate the within school analyses on free school meals (ie the interaction between group and free meals), we would first have to establish that the free meals effect varied between schools – expecting it to be **higher** in the RR schools – and then see if this variation could be explained by the group variable. In fact, the sample size and its structure (few observations within each school) mean that this is not a feasible analysis. The same applies to any analysis of the interaction between pre-test and group.

2.1 Diagnostic Pre-test Results
At pre-test, the control pupils are 0.47 sd units ahead ($\chi^2 = 5.19, 1, p < 0.03$). Those receiving free meals are 0.35 sd units behind ($\chi^2 = 8.14, 1, p < 0.005$). Of the total variation 42 per cent is variation between schools.

2.2 Progress: Book Level

About 47 per cent of the total variation is variation between schools. After controlling for the pre-tests (both the diagnostic test and initial book level), we find that the between school variation is reduced by about one third but is still important. After also controlling for ESL ($\chi^2 = 7.7, 1, p < 0.006$; ESL pupils make 2.6 levels or 0.35 sd units **more** progress) and free meals ($\chi^2 = 0.13, 1, p > 0.5$), we then find that group is important ($\chi^2 = 28.0, 1, p < 0.001$). The group effect is 6.3 book levels or 0.85 sd units and explains 54 per cent of the between school variation that remains after controlling for the other variables. However, some of the between school variation remains unexplained – about 30 per cent of all the residual variation.

2.3   Progress: Word Reading

The response variable here is the square root of the BAS at post-test.

About 31 per cent of the total variation is variation between schools. After controlling for the pre-tests (both the diagnostic test and initial word reading), we find that the between school variation is reduced by about 35 per cent but is still important. After also controlling for ESL ($\chi^2 = 13.7, 1, p < 0.001$; ESL pupils make 0.45 sd units **more** progress) and free meals ($\chi^2 = 1.7, 1, p > 0.5$), we then find that group is important ($\chi^2 = 33.7, 1, p < 0.001$). The group effect is 0.75 sd units and explains 62 per cent of the between school variation that remains after controlling for the other variables. However, some of the between school variation remains unexplained – about 18 per cent of all the residual variation.

2.4   Progress: Prose Reading

The response variable here is the square root of the Neale at post-test.

About 29 per cent of the total variation is variation between schools. After controlling for the pre-tests (both the diagnostic test and initial **word reading**), we find that the between school variation is reduced by about 36 per cent but is still important. After also controlling for ESL ($\chi^2 = 9.2, 1, p < 0.003$; ESL pupils make 0.39 sd units **more** progress) and free meals ($\chi^2 = 1.4, 1, p > 0.5$), we then find that group is important ($\chi^2 = 33.1, 1, p < 0.001$). The group effect is 0.82 sd units and explains 84 per cent of the between school variation that remains after controlling for the other variables. The remaining between school variation is very small.

2.5   Progress: Diagnostic Test

The response variable here is the Diagnostic Survey at post-test.

About 31 per cent of the total variation is variation between schools. After controlling for the pre-tests (both the diagnostic test, the square of the diagnostic test and initial **word reading**), we find that the between school variation is reduced by only about 11 per cent. After also controlling for ESL ($\chi^2 = 9.3, 1, p < 0.003$; ESL pupils make 0.39 sd units **more** progress) and free meals ($\chi^2 = 1.6, 1, p > 0.5$), we then find that group is important ($\chi^2 = 43.6, 1, p < 0.001$). The group effect is 0.94 sd units and explains 77 per cent of the between school variation that remains after controlling for the other variables. The remaining between school variation is very small.

2.6 Discussion

The following table summarises the results:

Variable	Overall
Book Level	0.85
Word Reading	0.75
Prose Reading	0.82
Diagnostic	0.94

The overall effects are somewhat greater than they are for the within school analyses, and the ordering is a little different with the effect for prose reading higher.

The strengths of the within school analyses are that school effects are controlled (at least to a degree), and interactions can be investigated. The weaknesses are the lack of randomisation, the possibility of 'contamination' of the control pupils by RR, and the small sample.

The strengths of the between school analyses are the larger sample and no possibility of contamination. The weaknesses are the absence of randomisation and hence the possibility of uncontrolled confounding variables associated with school (more serious than for the within school analyses where the allocation process is fairly clear even if not transparent), and the fact that interactions between RR and other variables cannot be investigated.

Despite all these caveats, it would be difficult not to conclude that RR has a substantial effect in the short term.

APPENDICES

3. Reading Recovery: within school analyses, second follow-up

These analyses are for the following outcomes:

1. BAS word reading;
2. Neale accuracy;
3. Neale comprehension;
4. BAS spelling.

Three subsets of the data (A,B,C) were considered for the time period from pre-test to second follow-up.

A. Pupils in those schools with both RR and control pupils, ignoring information on free school meals.

B. As (A), but only those pupils with no missing data on free meals at first <u>and</u> second follow up.

C. As (A), but only those pupils with data on free meals at first <u>or</u> second follow up.

3.1 Progress: pre-test to second follow-up

These results include data from those four pupils receiving the intervention in the second period.

A. There are 93 pupils in 16 schools, 60 RR pupils and 33 controls. A square root transformation was applied to each outcome to reduce skew. The pre-test variable used was the summed and standardised diagnostic test, as before. Sometimes the square of this test was needed in the regression equation. After allowing for the pre-test, all between school differences were extremely small and can be ignored.

The results are as follows:

Outcome	Effect size (sd units)	t statistic	p value
Word Reading	0.33	1.66	0.12
Neale Acc.	0.33	1.57	0.12
Neale Comp.	0.30	1.48	0.15
Spelling	0.18	0.88	0.40

Clearly, the overall effects are smaller than before, and are not statistically significant at conventional levels.

B. There are 81 pupils in 14 schools, 52 RR pupils and 29 controls. The free meals variable is operationalised as an ordered three category variable – none (n = 38), only at one occasion (n = 20), both occasions (n = 23) – to try to represent increasing levels of poverty. However, some of the pupils in the middle category could be there because of measurement error.

(i) Word Reading (Effect sizes, sd units)

Group	No fdin	One fdin	Both fdin	χ^2	p value
RR	0.29	0.61	0.92	7.4	0.03
Control	0.58	0.29	0		

(ii) Neale Accuracy (Effect sizes, sd units)

Group	No fdin	One fdin	Both fdin	χ^2	p value
RR	0.53	0.65	0.77	3.6	0.17
Control	0.64	0.32	0		

(iii) Neale Comprehension (Effect sizes, sd units)

Group	No fdin	One fdin	Both fdin	χ^2	p value
RR	0.58	0.65	0.76	3.8	0.15
Control	0.67	0.33	0		

(iv) BAS Spelling (Effect sizes, sd units)

Group	No fdin	One fdin	Both fdin	χ^2	p value
RR	0.11	0.36	0.61	3.6	0.17
Control	0.35	0.18	0		

Thus, pupils receiving free meals **and** RR make more progress and there is a gradient across the free meals variable. However, again, the effect is not as strong as it was for the first year.

APPENDICES
APPENDIX 4

C. The sample size etc is the same as in A. The free meals is just a dichotomy – received at least once (n = 45), did not receive at all (n = 48).

Outcome	Group	No fdin	Fdin	χ^2	p value
Word Reading	RR	0.40	0.74		
	Control	0.44	0	3.7	0.16
Neale Acc.	RR	0.59	0.71		
	Control	0.60	0	3.7	0.16
Neale Comp.	RR	0.56	0.60		
	Control	0.50	0	2.8	0.25
Spelling	RR	0.29	0.54		
	Control	0.44	0	3.1	0.22

The pattern of results is the same as in B, but the effects are less precisely estimated.

4. Reading Recovery: between school analyses, second follow-up

These results deal with progress over the two year period for all four outcomes.

The method of analysis is as described for the within school analysis.

4.1 Progress: pre-test to second follow-up.

These results are based on 223 pupils (145 controls and 78 RR) in 54 schools. Only schools with at least two pupils are included, and only pupils with data on free school meals at both occasions. Note that 'school' is defined by the **original** school the pupil was in.

At second follow-up, the RR pupils are just ahead of the control pupils on each of the four outcome measures.

For each outcome variable, a square root transformation was applied. For each analysis, the diagnostic test at pre-test and its square, BAS word reading at pre-test, and the ESL and free meals variables, were used as control variables.

Outcome	(a)	(b)	(c)
Word Reading	0.25	0.55	0.30
Neale Acc.	0.26	0.54	0.34
Neale Comp.	0.18	0.55	0.27
Spelling	0.21	0.70	0.42

APPENDICES
APPENDIX 4

(a) proportion of total variance between schools
(b) proportion of between school variance accounted for by control variables
(c) proportion of **remaining** between school variance accounted for by the group variable.

The effect sizes (sd units) are as follows:

Outcome	ESL	p value	Free meals	p value	Group	p value
Word Reading	0.57	0.001	0.12	0.29	0.37	0.007
Neale Acc.	0.53	0.001	0.16	0.15	0.41	0.005
Neale Comp.	0.34	0.02	0.20	0.11	0.30	0.04
Spelling	0.56	0.001	0.17	0.15	0.13	0.02

We see that the group effects are a little larger than they were for the within school analyses, and are statistically significant because of the larger sample. ESL pupils make more progress than non ESL pupils, the free meals effect (the difference between those receiving free meals at both occasions and those not receiving at all) is small.

5. Phonological Intervention: within school analyses, first follow-up

5.1 Progress: Phonological Tests

These results are based on 129 children in 23 schools.

Before controlling for pre-test, the post-test difference on the summed standardised Kirtley test is 0.24 units (s.e. = 0.17, t = 1.38, p > 0.16). After controlling for the Kirtley test and the Diagnostic Survey, the latter being the better predictor, the effect of the intervention is 0.32 SD units (s.e. = 0.15, t = 2.16, p < 0.04). The between school differences are small.

However, the effect of the intervention does appear to differ according to whether or not the child receives free school meals. After controlling for the pre-tests, the effect is 0.83 sd units for children receiving free school meals, -0.13 sd units for those who do not. Similar results are found if the pre-tests are excluded from the model: the corresponding effect sizes are 0.77 and -0.20 sd units. The proportion of children receiving free meals is essentially the same in the two groups and 42 per cent overall.

For the sound deletion test, the sub-tests were summed and the square root of the total used. The Kirtley pre-test did not predict the outcome but the Diagnostic Survey did. The intervention effect was 0.28 sd units (t = 2.1, p < 0.04). There was no evidence of the effect varying according to whether or not a child received free meals.

The correlation between the Kirtley and sound deletion tests was 0.55.

5.2 Progress: Reading Tests

The intervention effects, after controlling for the Diagnostic pre-test, are very small for each of book level, BAS reading (square root), Neale reading (square root) and the Diagnostic post-test.

It is interesting to note that for book level and the two reading tests, but not for the Diagnostic test, there appears to be an effect for children who have English as a second language (about 0.5 sd units) but not for those for whom English is their first language. However, there are only 18 ESL children in the sample and six of these are in one school and four in another. Hence the effect could well be confounded with between school differences in the effectiveness of the intervention, which this sample is too small to pick up. Also, if the Diagnostic pre-test is not included in the model, then the estimates of the effect of the intervention for the two language groups are all small. Hence, the interaction between intervention and language must be treated with great caution.

6. Phonological Intervention: between school analyses, first follow-up

6.1 Progress: Phonological Tests

These results are based on 197 (90 intervention, 107 control) children in 41 schools. Control children in RR schools were not included.

After controlling for the Kirtley pre-test and the Diagnostic Survey, the effect of the intervention on the Kirtley is 0.63 sd units (s.e. = 0.14, $t = 4.64$, $p < 0.001$). The group effect accounts for 67 per cent of the between school differences, the remaining between school differences being small.

For the sound deletion test, both the Kirtley pre-test and the Diagnostic Survey predict the outcome. The intervention effect was 0.49 sd units ($t = 3.0$, $p < 0.004$) and accounted for 58 per cent of the between school differences.

The correlation between the Kirtley and sound deletion tests was 0.52.

6.2 Progress: Reading Tests

The intervention effect, after controlling for the Diagnostic Survey pre-test, is very small for book level.

For the BAS (square root), the effect size is 0.21 sd units ($t=1.67$, $p < 0.10$) and this accounts for 7 per cent of the between school differences. For the Neale (again square root), the effect size is 0.18 sd units ($t = 1.56$, $p < 0.13$), accounting for 8 per cent of between school differences.

The effect is stronger for the Diagnostic Survey post-test : 0.36 sd units ($t=2.93$, $p < 0.004$), accounting for 25 per cent of the between school differences.

APPENDICES　　　　　　　　　　　　　　　　　　　　　　　　　　　　　　　　APPENDIX 4

7. Phonological Intervention: within school analyses, second follow-up

Essentially, these results show little effect of the intervention, either from the beginning of the study to second follow-up.

7.1 Progress: pre-test to second follow-up

There are 127 children – 86 intervention and 41 control – in 23 schools. The effects for all four reading tests, and for the two phonological tests are less than their standard errors when no pre-test controls are used (this is justified because of the random assignment).

All school effects were small. Square root transformations were applied to each reading test.

Controlling for the summed diagnostic test, and its square, at pre-test changes the results only slightly. The effects for the Neale accuracy and the Kirtley test are still less than their standard errors. For the other measures, we have:

Test	Effect size	CHI SQ	p value
Word Reading	0.15	1.5	0.22
Comp.	0.19	2.1	0.16
Spelling	0.17	1.8	0.19
Snowling	0.19	1.5	0.22

The effects of free dinners and first language were as follows:

Test	Free meals			ESL		
	Effect size	CHI SQ	p value	Effect size	CHI SQ	p value
Word Reading	0.18	1.48	0.23	0.31	3.14	0.08
Accuracy	0.27	3.35	0.07	0.28	2.4	0.13
Comp.	0.18	1.23	0.27	*		
Spelling	0.22	2.11	0.15	0.48	6.81	0.01
Kirtley	0.22	1.47	0.23	0.35	2.29	0.14
Snowling	0.18	1.02	0.32	*		

Note: * - Estimate less than its s.e.

There was no evidence of an interaction between free meals and the intervention on any outcomes.

APPENDICES

8. Phonological Intervention: between school analyses, second follow-up

These results are based on those children in the phonological and control schools, 41 schools altogether. They exclude all children in RR schools and the within school controls in phonological schools.

8.1 Progress: pre-test to second follow-up

There are 191 children, 86 Intervention and 105 Control.

The control variables used were: the diagnostic test at pre-test, its square (not needed for the Kirtley outcome), BAS at pre-test (not needed for the Kirtley) and the ESL variable (not needed for the Kirtley and less important for the Neale comprehension and Snowling). Free meals was important as a control variable only for the Kirtley.

Outcome	(a)	(b)	(c)
Word Reading	0.20	0.80	0.25
Neale Acc.	0.20	0.69	0.18
Neale Comp.	0.22	0.69	0.11
Spelling	0.21	0.70	0.24
Kirtle.	0.19	0.52	0.49
Snowling	0.19	0.54	0.33

(a) proportion of total variance between schools

(b) proportion of between school variance accounted by control variables

(c) proportion of remaining between school variance accounted for by the group variable.

Effect sizes are as follows:

Outcome	ESL	p value	Free meals	p value	Group	p value
Word Reading	0.52	0.001	*		0.27	0.03
Neale Acc.	0.44	0.003	*		0.21	0.10
Neale Comp.	0.22	0.15	*		0.19	0.17
Spelling	0.51	0.0005	0.19	0.11	0.26	0.05
Kirtley	*		0.31	0.04	0.39	0.008
Snowling	0.31	0.08	*		0.31	0.04

The group effects are a little higher, and the ESL effects a little lower, for the phonological tests than they are for the reading outcomes. Both the ESL and free meals effects are a little lower than they were for the RR between school comparisons. The group effects are similar in magnitude to those found at the first follow-up for the comparable tests, except for the Kirtley which is smaller.

REFERENCES

Adams, MJ *Beginning to Read: Learning and Thinking about Print*, The MIT Press, Cambridge MA (1990).

Allington, RL 'If they don't read much, how they ever gonna get good?', *Journal of Reading, 21*, 242-246 (1977).

Allington, RL 'Poor readers don't get to read much in reading groups', *Language Arts, 57*, 872-876 (1980).

Allington, RL 'The persistence of teacher beliefs in facets of the visual peceptual deficit hypothesis', *The Elementary School Journal, 82*, 351-359 (1982).

Allington, RL 'The reading instruction provided to readers of differing reading abilities', *The Elementary School Journal, 83*, 548-559 (1983).

Allington, RL 'Content coverage and contextual reading in reading groups', *Journal of Reading Behaviour, 16*, 85-96 (1984).

Allington, R and McGill-Franzen, A 'Children with reading problems: How we wrongly classify them and fail to teach many to read', *ERS Spectrum, 8*, 3-9 (1990).

Arter, J and Jenkins, J 'Differential diagnosis-prescriptive teaching: A critical appraisal', *Review of Educational Research, 49*, 517-555 (1979).

Audit Commission *Getting in on the Act: Provision for Pupils with Special Educational Needs: the National Picture*, HMSO, London (1992).

Barnes, JH and Lucas, H 'Positive discrimination in education: individuals, groups and institutions', in T Leggatt (ed.), *Sociological Theory and Survey Research*, Sage (1974).

Basic Skills, Adult Literacy and Basic Skills Unit, London (1994).

Becker, R and Gersten, R 'A follow-up of Follow Through: The later effects of the Direct Instruction Model on children in fifth and sixth grades', *American Educational Research Journal, 19*, 75-92 (1982).

Biemiller, A 'Relationships between oral reading rates for letters, words, and simple text in the development of reading achievement', *Reading Research Quarterly, 13*, 223-253 (1977-78).

Blatchford, P, Ireson, J and Joscelyne, T 'The initial teaching of reading: what do teachers think?', *Educational Psychology, 14 (3)*, 331-344 (1994).

Bond, GL and Dykstra, R 'The co-operative research program in first-grade reading instruction', *Reading Research Quarterly,2*, 5-142 (1967).

Bradley, L 'The Organisation of Motor Patterns for Spelling: an Effective Remedial Strategy for Backward Readers', *Developmental Medicine and Child Neurology, 23*, 83-91 (1981).

Bradley, L *Assessing Reading Difficulties: a Diagnostic and Remedial Approach*, 2nd edition, Macmillan, London and Basingstoke (1984).

Bradley, L 'Making Connections in Learning to Read and to Spell', *Applied Cognitive Psychology, 2*, 3-18 (1988).

Bradley, L and Bryant, P *Rhyme and Reason in Reading and Spelling*, University of Michigan Press, Ann Arbor (1985).

Bristow, PS 'Are poor readers passive readers? Some evidence, possible explanations, and potential solutions', *The Reading Teacher, 39*, 318-325 (1985).

Bruce, DJ 'The Analysis of Word Sounds', *British Journal of Educational Psychology, 34*, 158-170 (1964).

Bruner, J 'The transactional self' in J. Bruner and H. Haste (eds), *Making Sense: The Child's Construction of the World*, Methuen & Co., London (1987).

Bryant, P and Bradley, L *Children's Reading Problems*, Blackwell, Oxford (1985).

Butkowsky, S and Willows, D 'Cognitive-motivational characteristics of children varying in reading ability: Evidence for learned helplessness in poor readers', *Journal of Educational Psychology, 72*, 408-422 (1980).

Calfee, MC 'Assessment of independent reading skills', in A.S. Reber and D. Scarborough (eds), *Towards a Psychology of Reading*, Halstead Press, New York (1977).

Carroll, HC 'The remedial teaching of reading: an evaluation', *Remedial Education, 7 (1)*, 10-15 (1972).

Carter, LF 'The sustaining effects study of compensatory and elementary education', *Educational Researcher, 13*, 7, 4-13 (1984).

Chall, JS *Learning to Read: The Great Debate*, McGraw-Hill, New York (1967).

Chall, J *Stages of Reading Development*, McGraw-Hill, New York (1983).

Clay, MM *Reading: The Patterning of Complex Behaviour*, Heinemann, Portsmouth, NH (1979).

Clay, MM *The Early Detection of Reading Difficulties: A Diagnostic Survey with Recovery Procedures*, 3rd edition, Heinemann, Auckland, New Zealand (1985).

Clay, MM 'Implementing Reading Recovery: Systemic adaptations to an education innovation', *New Zealand Journal of Educational Studies, 22*, 35-58 (1987).

Clay, MM *Reading Recovery: A Guidebook for Teachers in Training*, Heineman, Auckland (1993).

Code of Practice on the Identification and Assessment of Special Educational Needs, Department for Education, London (1994).

Cohen, J, *Statistical Power Analysis for Behaviour Sciences*, Academic Press, New York (1977).

Daniels, JC and Diack, H *The Standard Reading Tests*, Chatto and Windus, London (1958).

Davie, R, Butler, N and Goldstein, H *From Birth to Seven*, Longman, London (1972).

Demetre, J D 'A Review of Evaluation Studies of the Reading Recovery Programme', *Report for National Curriculum Council* (1993).

Department of Education and Science *The Teaching and Learning of Reading: A Report by HMI*, HMSO, London (1991).

Donaldson, M and Reid, J 'Language skills and reading: A developmental perspective', in A. Hendry (ed.), *Teaching reading: The key issues*, Heinemann, London (1982).

Duffy, G and Anderson, L *Final report: Conceptions of reading project*. Unpublished report, Institute of Research on Teaching, Michigan State University (1981).

Dyer, PC 'Reading Recovery: A cost-effectiveness and educational-outcomes analysis', *Relevant Research for School Decisions, No. 2*, Educational Research Service, Arlington, VA (1992).

Elliot, CD, Murray, DJ and Pearson, LS *British Ability Scales*, NFER - Nelson, London (1984).

Entwisle, DR and Hayduk, LA *Early schooling: cognitive and affective outcomes*, Johns Hopkins University Press, Baltimore (1982).

Forell, ER 'The case for conservative reader placement', *The Reading Teacher, 35*, 857-862 (1985).

Frith, U 'Unexpected Spelling Problems' in U. Frith (ed) *Cognitive Processes in Spelling*, Academic Press, London (1980).

Frith, U 'Beneath the surface of developmental dyslexia', in K. Patterson, M. Coltheart and J. Marshall (eds), *Surface Dyslexia*, Lawrence Erlbaum Associates Ltd, London (1985).

Gambrell, LB, Wilson, RM and Gantt, WN 'Classroom observations of task-attending behaviours of good and poor readers', *Journal of Educational Psychology, 32*, 401-404 (1981).

Gaskins, IW, Downer, MA, Anderson, RC, Cunningham, PM, Gaskins, RW, Schomner, M and the Teachers of the Benchmark School 'A metacognitive approach to phonics: Using what you know to decode what you don't know', *Remedial and Special Education, 9* (1988).

Gersten, R and Carnine, D 'Direct Instruction mathematics: A longitudinal evaluation of low-income elementary school students', *The Elementary School Journal, 84(4)*, 395-407 (1984).

Gipps, C, Gross, H and Goldstein, H *Warnock's Eighteen per cent: Children with Special Needs in Primary Schools*, The Falmer Press, London (1987).

Gittelman, R and Feingold, I 'Children with reading disorders - 1. Efficacy of reading remediation', *Journal of Child Psychology & Psychiatry, 24*, 167-191 (1983).

Glynn, T, Crooks, T, Bethune, N, Ballard, K and Smith J *Reading Recovery in Context*, Dept of Education, Wellington, New Zealand (1989).

Goodman, K, Watson, B and Burke, C *Reading Miscue Inventory*, 2nd ed., Richard C Owen, New York (1987).

Goswami, U and Bryant, P *Phonological Skills and Learning to Read*, Lawrence Erlbaum Associates Ltd, London (1990).

Gregory, HM and Gregory, AH 'A Comparison of the Neale and the BAS Reading Tests', *Educational Psychology in Practice, 10 (1)*, 15-18 (1994).

Hatcher, P, Hulme, C and Ellis, AW 'Ameliorating early reading failure by integrating the teaching of reading and phonological skills: the phonological linkage hypothesis', *Child Development, 65*, 41-57 (1994).

Heath, SB *Ways with Words*, Cambridge University Press, Cambridge (1983).

Hewison, J and Tizard, J 'Parental involvement and reading attainment', *British Journal of Educational Psychology, 50*, 209-215 (1980).

Ireson, J, Blatchford, P and Joscelyne, T 'What do teachers do? Classroom activities in the initial teaching of reading', unpublished, London (1994).

Iversen, A and Tumner, W 'Phonological Processing Skills and the Reading Recovery Programme', *Journal of Educational Psychology, 85*, 112-126 (1993).

Johnston, PH and Winograd, PN 'Passive failure in reading', *Journal of Reading Behaviour, 17*, 279-301 (1985).

Jorgenson, G 'Relationship of classroom behaviour to the accuracy of the match between material difficulty and student ability', *Journal of Educational Psychology, 69*, 24-32 (1977).

Jorm, A, Share, D, McLean, R and Matthews, R 'Phonological recoding skills and learning to read: A longitudinal study', *Applied Psycholinguistics, 4*, 103-147 (1983).

Juel, C 'Learning to read and write: A longitudinal study of fifty-four children from first through fourth grade', *Journal of Educational Psychology, 80*, 437-447 (1988).

Kavale, K and Mattson, P "One jumped off the balance beam": Meta-analysis of perceptual-motor training', *Journal of Learning Disabilities, 16*, 165-173 (1983).

Kennedy, M, Birman, BF and Demaline, RF *The effectiveness of Chapter 1 services*, Office of Educational Research and Improvement, US Department of Education, Washington (1986).

Kirtley, C, Bryant, P, McLean, M and Bradley, L 'Rhyme, Rime and the Onset of Reading', *Journal of Experimental Child Psychology, 48*, 224 - 245 (1989).

LaBerge, D and Samuels, S 'Toward a theory of automatic information processing in reading', *Cognitive Psychology, 6*, 293-323 (1974).

Lazer, I, Hubbel, VR, Murray, H, Rosche, M and Royce, J *The persistence of preschool effects*, Department of Health, Education, and Welfare, Washington (1977).

LEA Audit of provision for children with Special Educational Needs (October, 1993)

Lundberg, I, Frost, J and Petersen, O 'Effects of an extensive program for stimulating phonological awareness in pre-school children', *Reading Research Quarterly, 23 (3)*, 263-284 (1988).

Lundberg, I, Olofsson, A and Wall, S 'Reading and Spelling skills in the First School Years predicted from Phonemic Awareness Skills in Kindergarten', *Scandinavian Journal of Psychology, 21*, 159-73 (1980).

Mann, V 'Why some children encounter reading problems', in J Torgesen and B Wong (eds), *Psychological and educational perspectives on learning disabilities*, Academic Press, New York, 133-159 (1986).

Mantzicopoulos, P, Morrison, D, Stone, E and Setrakian, W 'Academic effects of perceptually and phonetically based intervention for vulnerable readers', Paper presented at the American Educational Research Association, Boston (1990).

Maughan, B, Gray, G and Rutter, M 'Reading retardation and antisocial behavior: a follow-up into employment', *Journal of Child Psychology & Psychiatry, 26*, 741-758 (1985).

McGee, R and Share, DL 'Attention deficit-hyperactivity and academic failure: which comes first and what should be treated?' *Journal of American Academy of Child Psychology, 17*, 37-53 (1988).

Meyer, LA 'Long-Term Academic Effects of Direct Instruction Project Follow Through', *The Elementary School Journal, 84*, 380-394 (1984).

Mortimore, P, Sammons, P, Stoll, L, Lewis, D and Ecob, R *School Matters*, Open Books, Somerset, England (1988).

Nagy, WE and Anderson, RC 'How many words are there in printed school English?', *Reading Research Quarterly, 19*, 304-330 (1984).

Nagy, WE, Herman, PA and Anderson, RC 'Learning words from context', *Reading Research Quarterly, 20*, 233-253 (1985).

National Childhood Development Study, Adult Literacy and Basic Skills Unit, London (1987).

Neale, MD *Neale Analysis of Reading Ability*, revised, NFER-Nelson, Windsor (1988).

'New study finds scant reduction in New York school dropout rate', *New York Times*, May 15 1983.

Ofsted, *Reading Recovery in New Zealand: A report from the office of Her Majesty's Chief Inspector of Schools*, HMSO, London 1993.

Perfetti, CA *Reading Ability*, Oxford University Press, New York, 172-173, 195 (1985).

Pflaum, SW, Walberg, HJ, Karegianes, ML and Rasher, SP 'Reading instruction: A quantitative analysis', *Educational Researcher, 9*, 12-18 (1980).

Pinnell, GS, De Ford, DE and Lyons, CA *Reading Recovery: Early Intervention for At-Risk First Graders*, Educational Research Service Monograph, Virginia (1988).

Pinnell et al *The Reading Recovery Programme: Executive Summary 1984-91*, National Diffusion Network, USA (1991).

Pinnell, G, Lyons, C, DeFord, D, Bryk, A and Seltzer, M *Studying the Effectiveness of Early Intervention Approaches for First Grade Children Having Difficulty in Reading*, Martha L. King Language and Literacy Center Educational Report No. 16., Ohio State University, Columbus, OH (1991).

Pinnell, GS, Lyons, CA, DeFord, DE, Bryk, AS and Seltzer, M 'Comparing instructional models for the literacy education of high-risk first graders', *Reading Research Quarterly, 20(1)*, 9-39 (1994).

Plewis, I and Veldman, M 'Where does all the time go? Changes in pupils' experiences in Year 2 classrooms' in M. Hughes (ed.), *Teaching and Learning in Changing Times*, Blackwell, Oxford (1995).

Richman, N Stevenson, J and Graham, P *Pre-school to School: A Behavioural Study*, Academic Press, London (1982).

Rosenshine, B and Stevens, R 'Classroom instruction in reading', in P.D. Pearson, R. Barr, M.L. Kamil and P. Mosenthal (eds), *Handbook of Reading Research*, Longman, New York (1984).

Rutter, M 'A children's behaviour questionnaire for completion by teachers: preliminary findings', *Journal of Child Psychology and Psychiatry, 8*, 1-11 (1967).

Rutter, M *Helping Troubled Children*, Penguin, Middlesex (1975).

Rutter, M, Tizard, J and Whitmore, K *Education, Health and Behaviour*, Longmans, London (1970).

Rutter, M, Tizard, J, Yule, W, Graham, P and Whitmore, K 'Research report: Isle of Wight studies, 1964-1974', *Pyschological Medicine, 6*, 313-332 (1976).

Rutter, M, Cox, A, Tupling, C, Berger, M and Yule, W 'Attainment and adjustment in two geographical areas - 1. The prevalence of psychiatric disorder', *British Journal of Psychiatry, 126*, 493-509 (1975).

Schweinhart, LJ and Weikart, DP *A Summary of Significant Benefits: The High Scope Perry Pre-school Study Through Age 27*, Ypsilanti, Michigan; High Scope, UK (1993).

Shaver, JP and Nuhn, D 'The effectiveness of tutoring underachievers in reading and writing', *The Journal of Educational Research, 65*, 107-112 (1971).

Silver, AA, Hagin, RA and Beecher, R 'A program for secondary prevention of learning disabilities: Research in academic achievement and emotional adjustment', *Journal of Preventive Psychiatry, 1*, 77-87 (1981).

Spreen, O *Learning Disabled Children Growing Up,* Final Report to Health and Welfare, Child Health Programs Branch (1978).

Stanovich, KE 'Matthew effects in reading: Some consequences of individual differences in the acquisition of literacy', *Reading Research Quarterly, 21(4)*, 360-406 (1980).

Stanovich, KE 'Cognitive processes and the reading problems of learning disabled children: Evaluating the assumption of specificity', in J. Torgesen and B. Wong (eds), *Psychological and educational perspectives on learning disabilities,* Academic Press, New York, 87-131 (1986).

Stanovich, KE, Cunningham, AE and Cramer, B 'Assessing phonological awareness in kindergarten children: Issues of task comparability', *Journal of Experimental Child Psychology, 38,* 175-190 (1984).

Sternberg, R *Beyond IQ: A triarchic theory of human intelligence,* Cambridge University Press, New York (1985).

Stevenson, J and Fredman, G 'The social environmental correlates of reading ability', *Journal of Child Psychology and Psychiatry, 31 (5),* 681-698 (1990).

Stevenson, J Pennington, BF, Gilger, JW, DeFries, JC and Gillis, JJ 'Hyperactivity and spelling disability: testing for shared genetic aetiology', *Journal of Child Psychology and Psychiatry, 34 (7),* 1993 (1993).

Sticht, T 'Applications of the audread model to reading evaluation and instruction', in L.B. Resnick and P. Weaver (Eds), *Theory and practice of early reading,* Erlbaum, Hillsdale, NJ, 209-226 (1979).

Teale, WH 'Home background and young children's literacy development', in W.H. Teale and E. Sulzby (eds.) *Emergent Literacy: Writing and Reading,* Ablex Publishing Corporation, Norwood, NJ (1986).

Tizard, B, Blatchford, P, Burke, J, Farquhar, C and Plewis, I *Young Children at School in the Inner City,* Lawrence Erlbaum Assocs., Hove and London (1988).

Tizard, J, Schofield, WN and Hewison, J 'Collaboration between teachers and parents in assisting children's reading', *British Journal of Educational Psychology, 52,* 1-15 (1982).

Tunmer, WE 'Phonological processing skills and reading remediation', in C. Hulme and M. Snowling (eds.), *Reading Development and Dyslexia,* Whurr Publishers (1994).

Vygotsky, LS *Mind in Society: The Development of Higher Psychological Processes*, in M Cole, V John-Steiner, S Souber and E Souberman (eds. and trans.), Harvard University Press, Cambridge MA (1978).

Vygotsky, LS *Thought and Language*, The MIT Press, Cambridge, MA (1986).

Wadsworth, M *Roots of Delinquency*, Martin Robertson, Oxford (1979).

Walberg, HJ, Strykowski, BE, Royal, E and Hung, SS 'Exceptional performance', *Review of Educational Research, 54*, 87-112 (1984).

Walberg, HJ and Tsai, S 'Matthew effects in education', *American Educational Research Journal, 20*, 259-373 (1983).

Wasik, BA and Slavin, RE 'Preventing early reading failure with one-to-one tutoring: A review of five programs', *Reading Research Quarterly, 28 (2)*, 179-200 (1993).

Williams, S and McGee, R 'Reading attainment and juvenile delinquency', *Journal of Child Psychology and Psychiatry* (1994).

Wright, A 'Evaluation of the First British Reading Recovery Programme', *British Educational Research Journal, 18*, 351-368 (1992).

Yule, W and Rutter, M 'Reading and other difficulties', in M. Rutter and L. Hersov (eds.) *Child and Adolescent Psychiatry: Modern Approaches*, 2nd edition, Blackwell Scientific, Oxford (1985).